the states
of human
consciousness

the states
of human
consciousness

by **C. DALY KING**, M.A., Ph.D.

FOREWORD BY ROY FINCH

UNIVERSITY BOOKS *New Hyde Park, New York*

Distributed by:
H. A. HUMPHREY LTD.
5 Great Russell St., London, W.C.1

foreword

THE AUTHOR OF THIS BOOK died at his home in Bermuda just as he was finishing correcting the proofs. The book is a fitting valediction. In what he wrote here he had summed up the dominant interests and ideas of his life.

A trained scientist who refused to wear the blinkers of specialization, Daly King ventured widely off the beaten path. Like William James (and this book stands in the tradition of James's *Varieties of Religious Experience*), he was concerned with the borderlines of experience, with what lies beyond the everyday. It was said of James, when the question of putting up a memorial to him was discussed, that he could only be shown looking out the window. The same could be said of Daly King; he too was always "looking out the window." What concerned him most were the untried possibilities.

Yet Dr. King remained always the scientist, more like James's "tough-minded" than the "tender-minded." He never ceased to be the skeptical investigator, firmly committed to the methods of science, ever doubting what could not be established by experiment and logical proof. Often the scientist was not "scientific" enough for him; the scientist too fell victim to prejudices. Daly King had, in fact, little respect for the conventional or common opinion as such. His teachers Orage and Gurdjieff had convinced him that what most people believe is not, because of that, more likely, but rather less likely, to be true. The image of the true scientist as the "black sheep" appealed

v

to him. Such a "black sheep" questions and searches and refuses to follow the rest of the flock.

Dr. King had his advanced degrees in psychology from Columbia and Yale. He was born in 1895 and did his undergraduate work at Yale, graduating from there in 1916. After service in World War I and a brief career in business, he devoted himself to psychology and writing. His Ph.D. dissertation at Yale was on the subject of *Electromagnetic Studies of Sleep* (1946)[1], a subject which is discussed again in the present volume. He had previously written *Beyond Behaviorism* in 1927; *Integrative Psychology* (with W. M. and E. H. Marston) in 1931 and *The Psychology of Consciousness* in 1932.

In all these books there was discernible the influence of Orage and Gurdjieff, both of whom he saw for the first time in 1924, although he did not meet Gurdjieff personally until a few years later. With some trepidation, disliking anything bizarre or "occult," he joined a group which Orage was teaching in New York, based on Gurdjieff's ideas, and continued to study with Orage until Orage returned to England permanently in 1931. The Orage teaching he summed up in a book, privately printed in 1951, entitled *The Oragean Version*. In this book Dr. King states what had originally drawn him to Orage:

> I think what impressed me most at the first meeting was the complete and utter *rationality* of what I heard. ...The topics went to the heart of what had always intrigued me, those questions which I had always hitherto found hedged about by qualifications, half-statements, sometimes even a shamefaced avoidance, always a lack of specificity which had convinced me that the speaker didn't actually know the truth about such subjects. I was not merely fascinated; I received such an interior lift of pure exultation at the discovery that these questions could be considered seriously, fully and without equivocation, as had never occurred to me before and has never been as fully repeated since. To cap it all was the assurance of skepticism, the rational demand that I must *not* believe until I myself had obtained the proof.

[1]printed in *The Journal of General Psychology*, 1946, 35, 131-159.

✦ ✦ ✦

In the background of this present book, too, are the same figures of Orage and Gurdjieff, surely two of the most fascinating and unusual men of this century.

Alfred Richard Orage (parts of whose life have been described in books by Philip Mairet and Paul Selver) was a Yorkshireman born in 1873. He was close to the center of the British literary world as editor of the *New Age* in the years from 1907 to 1922. In 1921 he became acquainted with the teachings of Gurdjieff, through P. D. Ouspensky, and the following year, much to the consternation of many of his friends, sold the *New Age* and went to live in the Gurdjieff Institute at the Chateau du Prieurie in Fontainebleu. He taught the Gurdjieff ideas in New York until 1931 when he returned to England to launch the *New English Weekly*. He died in 1934.

Just before his death Orage said to a friend C. S. Nott (who reported it in a note appended to a collection of Orage's *Essays and Aphorisms* published in 1954): "You know, I thank God every day of my life that I met Gurdjieff."

Georges Ivanovitch Gurdjieff was born in 1877 of Greek ancestry in Alexandropol (now called Leninakan) near the Russian-Turkish frontier in what is now Russian Armenia. His early life, during which he embarked on a number of "journeys in search of truth," is described in an autobiographical work *Meetings with Remarkable Men,* published in English in 1963. After 1914 he taught in Moscow, Fontainebleu, London, Paris and New York, until his death in Paris in 1949.

What kind of a man was Gurdjieff? The question is unanswerable because there are as many answers as there were those who knew him.[2] The two men who made Gurdjieff's ideas most extensively

[2]Among those who have written about Gurdjieff and his ideas, in addition to Orage and Ouspensky, are: Maurice Nicoll, Rodney Collin, Kenneth Walker, Margaret Anderson, J. G. Bennett, Dorothy Caruso, Gorham Munson, Frank Lloyd Wright, Denis Saurat, Rene Daumal, Claude Bragdon, Dorothy Phillpotts, Rom Landau, and C. S. Nott. The most recent books are by Anderson, Walker and Nott.

known during his lifetime were Ouspensky and Orage but, although at one time or another he spoke highly of both, the question of how much they understood is complicated by the fact that he finally broke with each, for reasons which are also subject to various interpretations.

Daly King made no secret of the fact that he put the highest value on Orage's work and that, although the main ideas came from Gurdjieff, it was the genius of Orage which had put them in a coherent and intelligible form. This "Oragean Version" he regarded as essentially rational and "scientific," free from tinges of "mysticism" or "occultism." He was convinced that the Orage and Gurdjieff principles had nothing to fear from science and that, in fact, in the end they would be vindicated by science; and he set himself the task of relating them as closely as possible to scientific psychology, a task which culminates in the present book.

✦ ✦ ✦

The crucial thesis of this book is that, in addition to the forms of consciousness known to all human beings (here called Sleep and Waking), there exist two further forms, not yet widely known (here called Awakeness and Objective Consciousness). To establish this thesis Dr. King first attempts to define "consciousness" and to distinguish it from various "mental" activities. An earlier paper entitled *The Lockean Error in Modern Psychology* clarifies his thesis.[3] In that paper he maintained that the British philosopher John Locke had failed to distinguish between consciousness (taken as synonomous with awareness) and mental processes; and the results had been disastrous for the future history of psychology.[4] He wrote:

> ... there are not simply the "primary," "secondary" and "tertiary" qualities representing the "real" properties of "material

[3]The Journal of General Psychology, 1948, 38, 129-; 38
[4]The distinction, however, is clearly made by modern phenomenology, which has interesting points of comparison with the present book.

substances" and the sensory and emotional projections of the conscious entity upon those properties, but there are also the "quaternary" qualities representing the *mental* projections of the conscious entity upon the physical properties of those "material substances" that constitute a certain portion of the nervous system of the physical body.

Locke, in other words, confused "consciousness" with "thinking," failing to see that "Mental activity is fully homologous with emotional activity and with sensory activity." Until this error is corrected, Dr. King believed, there is no possibility of talking sensibly about "consciousness," which will always be confused with introspection.

Contrary to the introspectionist dogma of so much modern psychology, Dr. King believed that sensing, feeling and thinking *all* belong to the physiological nature of man, while consciousness should be thought of as the relation between an as-yet-undeveloped-subject and these physiological occurrences. To put the matter more crudely, *all* "mental" contents belong to an organism and not to a "subject," and the realization of this is the first step toward the development of a genuine "subject." The ultimate aim of what is described in this book is the "creation of a self," but this cannot be done until there is a fully experienced realization that there is as yet no "self."

What was it that led such an extremely skeptical man as Daly King, in the face of so much "common sense" conviction to the contrary and when anything "mystical" or "occult" was so naturally repugnant to him, to accept the unorthodox idea that additional states of human consciousness are possible? There were, I think, four main lines of evidence which convinced him.

The first was the example of Gurdjieff himself. At the beginning of Chapter VI of this book he writes:

>...Gurdjeff manifested himself in ways never elsewhere encountered by the writer, in ways so different from those of others that they constituted a plain and perceptible difference in level of existence upon his part. ...He is the only person ever met by the writer who gave the indubitable impression that all his

responses, mental, emotional and practical, were mutually *in balance* and thus the further impression that everyone else was out of step, but not this man himself. It is just what would be expected, though unpredictable, by a sophisticated Waking person when confronted by someone else in the state of Awakeness.

The second was his own experiences, particularly two of them described in the same chapter. As he recognizes, most psychologists and psychiatrists would probably regard these experiences as hallucinations. But Dr. King had the advantage of having studied hallucinations, and even of having experienced experimentally induced ones, and could report that the character of these two episodes was "utterly different from hallucinations." He was forced to believe that what he had experienced was *a new and different way of being aware, not to be confused in any way with merely thinking differently.*

A third type of evidence was furnished by his historical studies, and particularly his studies in Egyptology, which he discusses briefly in Chapter VII.[5] The more Dr. King studied the ancient Egyptians the more he became convinced that they, like some other ancient peoples, had known of the possibility of these additional states of consciousness. On this hypothesis he felt a great deal about them could be explained which would otherwise remain inexplicable. Dr. King rejected the notion that ancient peoples were "superstitious," an idea which he came to believe is merely a contemporary myth, flattering the modern ego. In the history of religions also (for example, in the Buddhist "enlightenment" and the Gnostic "experience of light") he found other evidences of spasmodic but decisive occurrences of the other forms of consciousness.

Finally, what is perhaps the most cogent line of evidence presented in this book, is what he felt was the inherent plausibility of his thesis within the area of psychology itself. Dr. King's point of view made it possible to admit fully both the claims of behaviorism and the counter-claims of the anti-behaviorists. The behaviorists, in his view (and even more the "cyberneticists") were entirely right in their

[5]This is also the subject of an unpublished manuscript on the history of Egypt.

description of the automatic and "passive" nature of ordinary experience. In holding that consciousness is not important and may be ignored they correctly described the situation, but the situation of present-day human beings. (In the terminology of this book "waking" consciousness only registers passively.) On the other hand, the opponents of behaviorism were also right in pointing out that consciousness *is* important, though they failed to recognize that this importance is *potential*. (Consciousness, in other words, *may* become "active.")

The common view that a human being is entirely the product of his heredity and environment is, for Daly King, an accurate description, more accurate than those who advance it realize. Many who accept it also accept the notion of a self-which-acts but, in fact, there is no such "self" as a third independent initiating factor. The key point of the book is that *a genuine self can only begin to appear if consciousness begins to be controlled from the side of a subject, and no longer merely registers passively the processes of an organism.* Self-awareness — or rather awareness of the organism and its processes — Daly King came to believe is the only point of potential transcendence in human beings, the only road by which the dictation of the organism to the (virtually non-existent) self can be broken.[6] As he phrased it:

> The novel, and indeed the sole, activity in which the subject himself can engage purely upon his own initiative is an active *awareness* of all the aforementioned processes.

The similarities between the hypnotic state and ordinary consciousness had impressed Dr. King for many years. So had the analogy between "waking from sleep" and "waking from ordinary consciousness" described in religious literature. As a psychologist, he came to believe that what Oriental thought, in particular, had described as "waking from the dreams of life" could be described in psychological terms as becoming aware of the present purely automatic functioning

---

[6]In taking consciousness as the point of potential transcendence, rather than the will or spirit, Orage and King were closer to the Eastern religious tradition than to the Western.

of the organism-in-its-environment. The automatic stimulus-and-response circuits which dominate our lives are — or rather supply — the "dreams of life."

The Orage-Gurdjieff teaching proposes a way of self-development through the only leverage available — self-awareness. The method is a subtle but ruthless detachment of consciousness from its identification with the habitual behaviors of the organism, *including* the behaviors of thinking and acting. Only those who have some inkling of how much they are "victims of themselves," of course, would wish to make the effort; others — the vaster majority — know nothing about themselves at all.

What is distinctive in the Orage-King emphasis, and particularly emphasized by Dr. King, is the insistence that, if the whole procedure is not to disintegrate into a quagmire of introspection, what has to be observed first and foremost is the *physical organism*. Dr. King repeatedly declared that there is nothing of ourselves about which we *can* be objective except our physical responses and behaviors. The attempt to observe one's feelings and thoughts actually leads to complicated forms of self-deception. "Knowing oneself" means, first of all, becoming aware of one's physical behavior and then, only secondarily and at a very advanced stage, becoming aware objectively of one's feelings and thoughts.

Dr. King never minimized the extreme difficulty of this "objectivizing of ourselves" or the likelihood (in fact, he felt the virtual certainty) that such attempts would in most cases lead only to forms of neurosis. He always insisted that nothing could be done without proper help and guidance. Yet he also felt that along this path lay the only possibility of fundamental human change.

✦ ✦ ✦

It is a truism repeated *ad nauseum* that human beings have changed everything but themselves. Social revolutions repeatedly run afoul of this intransigence of human nature — the weakness, vanity,

power-and-status-seeking which vitiate so many hopes. With techno-
logical knowledge we are now finally tempted to resort to chemicals
or various forms of "human engineering" to alter what is now called
the "human material."

Yet, as Daly King recognized, this would be an evasion, for what
we want is not to *be* changed (at least not by other people who have
no genuinely superior ground from which to do it), but to change
ourselves — that is, to bring about the change ourselves from within.

In an age which seeks to objectify and bring to consciousness
what formerly controlled us unconsciously, (and that is, in a sense,
the common denominator of Freud and Marx and others), the suggestion that we recognize as the most basic example of estrangement
just our average everyday behavior is the most modern of ideas. Sub-
stituting conscious control for unconscious alienation will never be
radical enough until we recognize that it is just in our so-called
normal, daily behavior that we are most estranged and most
uncontrolled.

This fact, hidden by its very omnipresence, is much harder to see
than the effects of unconscious economic or libidinal determinations.
More than of social or sexual forces we are in the grip of an illusory
idea of ourselves, and every tendency of pride, fear, training and convention conspires to keep us there. We are willing to change our
ideas, but not ourselves, because we are scarcely aware that we *are*
more than our ideas.

The change begins, as the present book emphasizes, in the recog-
nition of the fundamental difference between knowledge and being.
What we *are* is still something different from what we *know,* and to
know a great deal guarantees nothing about the level of our being.
To develop our being, and not merely to accumulate knowledge or
power — this remains the true human task.

ROY FINCH

July, 1963
Sarah Lawrence College

contents

FOREWORD BY ROY FINCH   v

INTRODUCTION   The Origins of the Investigation   1

CHAPTER I   A Scientific Analysis of the
Problem of Consciousness   11

CHAPTER II   The Activation of Consciousness   29

CHAPTER III   The States of Consciousness   45

CHAPTER IV   Sleep   53

CHAPTER V   Waking   81

CHAPTER VI   Awakeness   99

CHAPTER VII   Objective Consciousness   131

CHAPTER VIII   The Outcome of the Investigation   155

INDEX   169

introduction

THE ORIGINS
OF THE INVESTIGATION

THE SUBJECT OF THIS BOOK is given succinctly in its title. Its purpose is to discuss and, so far as possible, to describe the various states of consciousness potentially within the experience of human beings. Even in the later and more speculative chapters these questions are formulated from the viewpoint of the scientist.

Therefore, in the present section and elsewhere, other matters are mentioned only in relation to the main theses of the book and will not be discussed outside that connotation. By this means many irrelevant digressions will be avoided, such as the writer's personal estimation of psychoanalysis, any general exposition of the ideas and disciplines of the Gurdjieff Institute formerly at Fontainebleau in France and, in Chapter VII, a detailed investigation of the religious concepts of the ancient Egyptians. Such topics are introduced only insofar as they refer specifically to the present subject-matter.

With all of these problems other writers have dealt extensively and this one, also, has treated of them: for example, in *Integrative Psychology,* Harcourt Brace, 1931; *The Psychology of Consciousness,* Harcourt Brace, 1932; *The Oragean Version,* privately, 1951; and

1

Heritage, A Social Interpretation of the History of Ancient Egypt, not yet published.

Accordingly this first short section is autobiographical only to the extent of its relevance to the subject of the book. But it is felt that the reader should be acquainted with the author's background and experience in relation to the matters to be discussed and thus be better able to form his own conclusions as to any personal idiosyncrasies that may be involved; in any case, to realize the origins of the view to be expressed.

A small volume entitled *The Psychology of Insanity* by Bernard Hart, published in 1912, aroused the writer's first serious interest in this subject. Dr. Hart was a thinker whose sagacity has been too little appreciated amid the tumults arising later; he was an announced subjectivist but one who understood the objectivist position and could formulate it clearly, an ability too often lacking in the usual proponent of subjectivist concepts. He dealt in terms such as complex, suppression, unconscious mental process and so on, which he asserted to possess a real significance but which, he was careful to point out, could "lay no claim to phenomenal reality". Philosophically he was a parallelist to the extent that he appears to have held the opinion that all the phenomena of consciousness were accompanied by corresponding neurological phenomena in the organism's brain, but without our being able to establish the explicit connection between the two parallel series of events. With these neurological phenomena he did not concern himself but only with what he called the psychological phenomena that accompanied them, with the laws which the latter followed and which he felt could be formulated in purely psychological terms lacking any physiological reference.

The present writer thus began his career as a subjectivist in his investigation of consciousness and soon became so interested in the subject that he decided to submit himself to the full subjectivist treatment and to probe the matter thoroughly. To this end during the years, 1922-1923, he underwent a personal psychoanalysis under Dr. Edward J. Kempf, then a practitioner of the technique in New York City. Dr. Kempf, of course, was a subjectivist also, in that he took the analogical terms of psychoanalysis perfectly seriously. But he was not quite the same sort of subjectivist as Dr. Hart, for his idea was not simply that the psychological events with which he dealt, were accompanied by the neurological phenomena of the autonomic nervous system but that in fact they were *due* to the latter.

Also at this time the present writer did much reading of mystical and semi-mystical works, such as those of Bucke, Eriksen and Steiner, and he even began a resolute investigation of the complexities of the really ancient Egyptian religion in the hope of discovering what those very remarkable people might have to say on the question.

In 1927 and 1928 he returned to the academic fold and studied psychology professionally at Columbia University under Dr. William M. Marston, submitting a thesis entitled "An Experimental Study of the Psychonic Theory of Consciousness". He received an M.A. degree and immediately afterwards collaborated with Dr. Marston on a book called *Integrative Psychology* which put forward the latter's important viewpoint regarding both behavioral and experiential phenomena.

At this period Dr. John B. Watson was the leading exponent of Behaviorism and the writer took advantage of an acquaintance with him to discuss the question of the nature of consciousness. Dr. Watson, though a very friendly person and certainly a very competent scientist, showed little interest in this question; indeed he maintained that scientifically the term, consciousness, had no genuine meaning, that it was superfluous and gratuitous and that it would be better to disregard it entirely in any scientific investigation. In other words, he was an advanced objectivist in his position.

But if Dr. Watson was objectivist, Dr. Marston was even more so. He asserted that consciousness was both to be defined and to be identified in purely objective terms as a particular kind of physical energy, specifically as psychonic energy, which was continually being produced at the synapses of the nervous system during the integration of the nervous impulses there being combined. He disagreed with the behaviorist position that consciousness existed only as a catchword or delusional postulation, indeed he thought consciousness to be the most important factor in the whole human economy; but what he meant by consciousness was a *thing,* explicitly it was a form of electrochemically formulable energy, constantly manufactured within the organism itself. Although this writer did not agree completely with Dr. Marston, at that time he had become an objectivist himself and he was so sympathetic with these ideas that he was invited to, and did, write the chapters in Dr. Marston's book that dealt with consciousness and its resultant phenomena, namely sensation, thought process and emotion. Dr. Marston's position was certainly objectivist and, since this writer has formulated it to the satisfaction of its deviser, he feels fully qualified to discuss that viewpoint.

Integrative Psychology was published in 1931. During the following ten years the events of life precluded any further scientific work, although much reading on these subjects continued, but in 1941 the writer returned to Yale University (where he had spent his undergraduate years) and matriculated as a postgraduate student in psychology. As many as possible of his courses were taken at the Yale School of Medicine and there he met Dr. Harold Saxton Burr under whom he studied neurology for a number of terms. In 1943 he was accorded the degree of M.A. and in 1945 that of Ph.D. Naturally Dr. Burr was an objectivist who believed that very many of the phenomena of consciousness already could be correlated exactly with neurological event and that eventually the same would apply to all of them. This did not mean, however, that he embraced the view of parallelism; to Dr. Burr, as to most of the medical profession, the neurological event, in the visual cortex for instance, is *identical with* the sensation of blue experienced by the subject. Another of the brilliant researchers whom the writer has been fortunate to have known, Dr. Burr was able to formulate his objectivist position with great clarity. Nevertheless, there is bound to remain something unsatisfactory to the psychologist in the idea that the neurological event *is* the sensation; this is too much like saying that the pulling of the trigger is identical with the shot from the gun's barrel or even with the hit on the target. In both series of events there exist very close connections between the parts comprising them, there may even be cause-and-effect connections, but nonetheless essential distinctions remain to be made. Meantime the writer was pursuing the usual courses in a medical school—physiology, neuroanatomy, brain dissections and so on. His doctoral thesis was titled Electrometric Studies of Sleep and established the relation between the steady-state DC field of the human body and the various degrees of the sleeping state of consciousness as measured by the concurrent AC electroencephalograms. No subjective reports were taken and this work was wholly objective.

The activities reported so far have been academic and almost stodgily respectable but now another source of information is to be mentioned, perhaps not so highly regarded by academicians, although it is the most important of all. In 1924 the writer encountered an organization whose headquarters were at Fontainebleau in France and which went under the unusual name of The Institute for the Harmonious Development of Man. Such, as it were, extracurricular organizations must be approached with a strict scepticism but the Institute itself demanded that precise attitude upon the part of its students and possessed the means to assure itself that the attitude was taken by them in fact. No difficulties of such a nature were interposed.

The founder and director of the Institute was M. Georges Ivanovitch Gurdjieff; and the writer has no hesitation in calling him one of the hundred, perhaps one of the fifty, most remarkable men known to us in our history. Although he did not claim personally to have discovered all of it, the mere range of his knowledge was so far beyond that of others as to make comparisons not merely invidious but impossible. His methods of instructing his pupils were highly individual and highly unusual and one of his principles seemed to be to guard against their acquirement of too much knowledge prematurely; a corresponding degree of understanding was to be demanded and, until it had been attained, additional knowledge was inadvisable. There was also the Institute prohibition against belief or credulity; information, and especially psychological information, must be confirmed by the student personally before he was entitled to assume that it was correct.

To the ordinary inquirer such a man cannot fail to present what at first seem to be extraordinary contradictions. M. Gurdjieff was the most extreme objectivist of all those met by the author; he went so far as to maintain that everything in the entire universe is material in the usual sense of possessing physical mass, and this included human thoughts, emotions, concepts and reason itself. On the other hand he stood in no awe of esotericism and many of the propositions of the Institute were of a nature that would commonly be called esoteric. However, the explanation of these propositions was far from the usual esoteric one.

M. Gurdjieff's attitude toward devils was typical of his attitude toward the kind of credulous questions that were often addressed to him: he asserted that no such creatures or forces existed in the universe, and that the idea of devils was but the romantic invention of irrational romanticists. Since certain of his questioners considered him quite capable of magics of his own and were not too sure just how snowy they might be, this also appeared to them as a contradiction.

Such a man, despite all his precautions, is bound to arouse a superstitious reverence on the part of many of his followers, just as he must elicit ignorant rejoinders and the charge of charlatanism from his opponents. To the best of his knowledge the present writer was able to avoid adopting both of those tendencies, although he knew M.

Gurdjieff personally over a considerable number of years. But his own instruction came primarily from Mr. Alfred Richard Orage, the representative of the Institute in the United States (with headquarters in New York City), by whom he was later accredited as an instructor of the Institute and so served for some four or five years.

Mr. Orage was the leading literary critic of his day in England, sometime editor of the *New Age* and later of the *New English Weekly,* both of them London periodicals. He was the most brilliant of all the intellectualists whom the writer has known, a man of warm and comprehensive sympathies, and a close personal friend until his death in 1934.

It was solely Orage's exposition that enlightened the writer concerning the many and extraordinarily penetrating propositions of the Institute and his debt to the former is very great. Especially is this so in regard to our present subject, for the Institute held the key to the subtle and baffling problem of the real nature of consciousness, the key that resolves the subjectivist-objectivist contradiction, and which, if mastered and understood, provides a genuine solution for this perplexing puzzle. Academic work revealed the nature of the problem but only the invaluable assistance of Orage made possible the writer's understanding of the answer.

Mr. Orage returned to England in 1931 but work of this sort continued for the writer thereafter; it had begun in 1924 and it may be said to have concluded finally with the death of M. Gurdjieff in 1949. Since then he has had no connections with the successor Institute, with the Gurdjieff Foundation in New York nor with the many groups both in the United States and abroad that now carry on activities which in his opinion are no longer intellectually or emotionally in the genuine tradition of the original Institute. Naturally the last statement is open to dispute, and no doubt shall be disputed, by those who feel otherwise; but it seems only proper here to state the view of the writer.

However, a number of the propositions of the original Institute will form a part of this book and will be identified as such at the relevant places in the text. And since the author is a scientist himself, he is aware that some of these propositions are in advance of modern scientific research, chiefly perhaps because they have been drawn in part from past civilizations that on their own account performed a great deal of research during their long histories.

No sane man wishes to disparage modern research and the very considerable amount of impartial investigation it has accomplished. But certainly we of today have not solved every problem and science is far from a completed discipline. There is more to learn than we have yet learned, and the first one to make this acknowledgement is the scientist himself. If science knew everything, it would be redundant to educate any more scientists, for the task would have been finished. Scientists don't think it has been, by a long throw. Thus to say that certain propositions may be ahead of scientific knowledge, is by no means a phantastic or ignorant assertion; it is simply one that needs to be examined carefully and non-credulously.

When that has been done, the position of this book will turn out to be neither subjectivist nor objectivist psychologically. Nor can it be called a combination of the two viewpoints, for it is surely not in the nature of their additive sum. Perhaps it might be called an integration of the two views, as water is an integration of hydrogen and oxygen or as the psychological response of captivation is an integration of active inducement and passive submission. To carry the analogy further, the present position might be said to represent an integration of active objectivism and passive subjectivism. But, like all integrations, it is typical of neither of its components.

Whatever it may be called, it subsumes what probably may be the final conclusions of the writer on the nature and possibilities of human consciousness, which he has studied for many years. He has earlier published two books on this subject (*Beyond Behaviorism*, 1927, and *The Psychology of Consciousness*, 1932) as well as a number of articles contributed to the technical journals; but none of these embody the full statement of the findings now reached. The latter are offered not as undeniable verity but in the hope that they may be of assistance to others equally interested in the problem.

chapter I

A SCIENTIFIC ANALYSIS OF THE PROBLEM OF CONSCIOUSNESS

CONSCIOUSNESS IS A VAGUE TERM, very vaguely defined. In fields other than the scientific it can mean almost anything and, even in scientific usage, its significance is deplorably unrigorous. Nevertheless, the term raises a scientific problem, if only because the steps involved in the scientific method—observation, induction, deduction and, once again, observation of results—all require what by common consent we are accustomed to call consciousness upon the part of the experimenter.

But although we consent in common to call this 'something' consciousness, our lack of definition results in disagreement upon the real nature of this 'something-called-consciousness.' Some of us deny flatly that it is anything at all or even exists; others, in more sophisticated fashion, identify consciousness loosely with introspection or with some other form of thought process; and our supersophisticates speak confidently (albeit with occasional self-contradictions) about the preconscious, the subconscious, the foreconscious, the unconscious, and the like. For the moment we prefer to leave these last terms out of the discussion and to consider, instead, the three contrasting and long-established views as to the nature of consciousness itself.

The first idea is that consciousness constitutes the primary reality and that the structures by or through which it is mediated—the nerv-

11

ous system, earlier the heart and sometimes the blood stream—are secondary, originating in some way from the prior existence of the very consciousness of which they are only appendages. The second is that the mediators of consciousness are the primary factors and that it is due to their operations that consciousness arises in the first place, being a result or by-product of neural or other similar phenomena. The third view states that neither of the above contrasts can be considered as primary, that we must recognize the equal existence of the two sets of phenomena, the purely psychological and the purely physiological, but that for the purposes of rational discussion and scientific investigation these two categories of events must be kept strictly within two separate worlds of discourse, each being described in its own appropriate terms, which in the two cases will never have any legitimate cross-references. This last position is called parallelism; it admits the simultaneous existence of the psychological and the physiological trains of events and that there in fact may be close sequential correspondences between them but states that we are unable to say that either is caused by the other or to trace any specific connection between them.

All of these views have some real merit and contain a portion of real insight, as we shall see when we come to their eventual reconciliation. But the parallelist position, although seemingly the most broadminded, is actually the least satisfactory, for at bottom it is only a stop-gap view of immediate expediency, seeking a pseudo-reconciliation between the opposing positions from which it has been derived and doing so, moreover, by what looks suspiciously like a begging of the question. Thus it is said that neurological phenomena are accompanied by conscious phenomena, or vice versa, but that we are unable to state which occurs first, whether there be some causal relationship in one direction or the other, or indeed just what the connection between them may be. At one time no doubt all this was true and, if it were still true, the argument would be far better grounded than it is. For it rests upon alleged inability that is no longer the case; and when the inability has vanished, so has the argument that rests upon it.

Our own view will be that the term, consciousness, refers always and legitimately only to the *relationship* between the subjective entity, or experiencer, and those end-products of the neural functioning of his body which furnish the experiencer with what in fact he experiences. This is why the word, consciousness, is so difficult for most people to grasp and why its connotations are vague, often self-contradictory and sometimes even meaningless. Most of us are unaccustomed to thinking in terms of field theory and we are unaware that *three* forces, not merely two, are present in all phenomenal occurrence.

When experience occurs, there is certainly 1) an experiencer and there is 2) something that furnishes his experience to him. That something is precisely the operations of his nervous systems. But there is also a third factor involved: it is 3) the relationship existing between the experiencer and the neural raw material from which his experiences result. And this relationship determines the extent and the type of consciousness operative in the given instance.

That will become clearer later. At this point we must notice that the above definition of consciousness has not as yet been defended adequately, and we wish to inquire what the scientist who admits the fact of his own consciousness, means when he admits it. It is a thesis of this chapter that what he means, is fairly simple. And it is a further thesis that most unexpected implications lie embedded in that meaning.

When the scientist informs his colleague, "I observed the following readings in millivolts," he often means that he has noted certain markings of a stylus upon graph paper or perhaps the numbers indicated by the end of a variable pointer. The key words are *I* and *observe*. It will be agreed that the observation is a function of the scientist's organism, chiefly of its optical apparatus and partly also of its mental and recent-memory mediators. These apparatuses are neurological in nature and the end-products of their diverse operations supply the observational data in question. But to whom are these data supplied? Who is the "I" of the scientist's first remark?

It is a mistake, we can see, to identify the experiencer with that which supplies the experience, the I with the It or associated body. There are a number of reasons for this statement, none of them mystical. For example, the organism has a name and address, neither of them necessarily permanent; it is also continually passing through various states or conditions, some of them basically different, in their own descriptive terms, from others. But the term, I, has a permanence, however artificial, which the man himself will claim if he is forced to consider the matter. I am the same I—he will tell you—who was depressed yesterday but am happy today, who observed the football game as well as the millivolt readings, who was asleep last night but am awake this morning.

By the same token it has been pointed out many times that an "I" as variable as all that is not much of an "I"; and when it is noticed that the variations of "I" bear a one-to-one correspondence with the variations of the organism, it has been asserted that "I" is no more than a delusion and refers really to the body itself. But this sort of hasty mis-thinking cannot properly meet the case for, aside from the fact that it is the variations and not the "I" which refer directly to the body, it remains true that there is a continuing self-identification with a constantly varying organism: that the same "I" remembers his drunkenness when he is sober and sometimes his nocturnal dreams when he is awake. Aldous Huxley once asserted that memory and the confused swarm of ideas enclosed within the slowly changing spatio-temporal cage of the body certainly do not constitute a viable soul. But just as certainly they would appear to constitute what most people mean by the term, I.

We then may say that "I" constitutes the core of subjectivity in the case of the human being. We may also take it as a premise that "I" is an entity postulated automatically by the given human being in order to account for consistency amid variability, the idea of which originates primarily from the memory function.

Originally, therefore, "I" is a postulated entity. This fact of postulation, however, is not necessarily a discredit to it; the term, electron, was once also just such a postulated entity. But it is true that the sort of "I" of which we have been speaking possesses no undue amount of objectivity; and so we shall write it as I_0. And already, for the naive, there has been set up the dualism or dichotomy of I and It, of the experiencer and the body that supplies the experience. Let us guard against that naiveté ourselves. We must reflect that in all real phenomena there are always present three separate factors or forces, and that in the present case the third factor is immediately apparent. This third factor is just the relation existing between I and It, the relation which in itself constitutes a certain type of consciousness. Let us first consider the general type of this relationship which we shall later propose to define as one kind of consciousness.

When we said that it was a mistake to identify the experiencer with that which supplies the experience, we were also calling attention to the fact that the experience *is* supplied—by the end-products of the neurological functioning of the organism. And since the experiencer has not even a notion as to what the experience shall be until already it has been manufactured in the nervous system centers, it is therefore what is called a "determined" experience. The concept that the experiencer—I_0—can *in any way* control it, is simply a delusion, often arising from the circumstance that, under certain conditions, some part of the total neurological system does successfully oppose (and thus control) some other part of the same system, thereby giving rise to an artificial experience of control at second hand, as it were. But in all such cases, some of which can exemplify a considerable subtlety, it remains that the real activity is always on the neurological side of the equation, never on the experiencing side, which latter remains genuinely passive throughout.

To illustrate this loosely we can say, in respect of the occurence of experience, that about 99 44/100 per cent of the phenomenon takes place neurologically and includes all of the involved activity, while a mere 56/100 per cent occurs on the part of the experiencer, and that this tiny portion consists exclusively of an only passive registration of what has just previously gone forward neurologically in the organism. Diagrammatically we have the following simple situation:

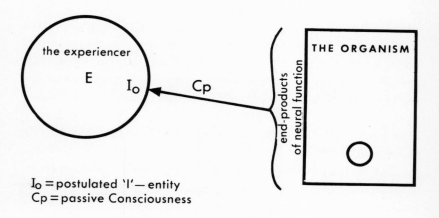

I_o = postulated 'I'— entity
C_p = passive Consciousness

DIAGRAM I

A fuller analysis of this arrangement will prove of value. Experience falls into three plainly differentiable categories: sensory, emotional and mental; and these correspond exactly with the ascertained major neurological divisions of the organism's nervous system.

When a sensory experience takes place, the following general conditions precede it:

1. energy external (or on some occasions internal) to the organism impinges upon some end-organ (receptor) of the organism;

2. the impinging energy is integrated with the organic energy already present in the receptor;

3. the resultant impulse is conducted along a nerve tract to the first synapse;

4. there it is integrated with similar impulses and undergoes modifications characteristic of synaptic conduction;

5. this resultant impulse, now of the second transmittory degree, is again conducted along a nerve tract to the second synapse, in the thalamus, and thence by a third-order neurone to the primary arrival platform in the cortex;

6. and is conducted along another nerve tract to a cortical location which comprises its final arrival platform;

7. it is there combined with similarly arriving impulses;

8. at this spatio-temporal point it becomes, not the experience, but the raw material of a sensory experience.

When an emotional experience occurs, the following general conditions precede it:

1. impulses from sensory or other regions impinge upon the basal ganglia of the organism;

2. there they undergo synaptic integration with previous impulses within the ganglia themselves;

3. and are projected along nerve tracts to the cortex;

4. here further integration takes place;

5. and the resultant impulses are conducted to the motor centers of the organism;

6. where they are integrated with the constant tonic discharge of the organism;

7. these integrations, now on their way to the musculature of the organism, pass through, or in any case influence, the basal gangliar region from which they originated;

8. at this spatio-temporal point they become, not the experience, but the raw material of an emotional experience.

When a mental experience occurs, the following general conditions precede it:

1. sensory and basal gangliar impulses, already complexly integrated, impinge upon the correlation centers of the cortex;

2. there they are integrated synaptically with the previous impulses already present in these centers;

3. the resultant impulse-series is conducted along correlation or association nerve tracts to further correlation centers in the cortex;

4. where it is combined synaptically with similar impulse-series arriving from other cortical locations;

5. these combinations then are transmitted to yet more complex correlation centers, chiefly of the frontal lobes of the cortex;

6. where they undergo further integration;

7. and their results are then ready for transmission (and may be transmitted) either to the motor centers of the cortex or, in the case of some 67 per cent of them,

to the cerebellum where, so far as concerns present research, they vanish; the pathway for cerebellar vestibular reflexes originates from the inner ear, not from the cortex;

8. at the preceding spatio-temporal point they become, not the experience, but the raw material of a mental or intellectual experience.

Sensory stage 8, motor or basal gangliar stage 8 and correlation stage 8 furnish those end-products of the organism's neural functioning which constitute the raw material of all our present ordinary human experience. The end-products of neural function consist of integrated nerve-impulse-groups whose ultimate nature is solely electrochemical and is fully formulable in the terms and equations of a completed science of physics. They comprise entirely objective phenomena and include no aspect whatever either of subjectivity or of subjective experience.

Nevertheless, experience occurs. And it can be demonstrated in the laboratories of physiological psychology that such sensory experiences correspond in the most detailed ways just to sensory stage 8, above mentioned. As both clinical investigation and experiment show, when some defect is caused in the functioning of the sensory nervous system of the organism, either accidentally or deliberately, a correlated deficit occurs in the experience of the subject. This deficit specifically diminishes the consciousness of the subject (by withholding certain material from him), with the result that what the subjective entity registers in his experience, is reduced comparably. The effect is not upon the subject, whose characteristics remain the same, but instead it is upon consciousness, the third force or factor in the phenomenon of subjective experience.

Our reasoning processes, as well as clinical demonstrations (although perhaps not yet as complete as in the sensory case), bring us to the conviction that emotional and mental experiences bear the same one-to-one correspondence with neurological event as in the case of the sensory category. In the latter instances, of course, the correspondences are with basal gangliar stage 8 and with correlation stage 8 respectively.

But the very terms of this analysis, in addition to our common sense, must assure us that it is necessary to differentiate between the end-products of neural functioning upon the one hand and, upon the other, the corresponding experiences to which they give rise.

This distinction can be made clear by postulating the experiencer, E, whose relation to the organism, O, consists in the relating term, C_p, signifying a passive consciousness and meaning that the subjective entity, I_O, must experience only what is so furnished by O, represented in this case by the end-products of O's neural functions. Thus we see that I_O, which is postulated undeliberately by the ordinary man for the purpose of explaining his vague self-identification, is equally demanded rationally by a careful analysis of the scientific problem of the nature of consciousness.

And thus, to paraphrase a Lockean formulation, a human being —as distinguished from a merely human organism—may be defined as a three-termed relationship such that the first (and active) term comprises the threefold end-products of the neural functioning of the human organism, the second (and passive) term comprises the experiencer of the results of the first term, and the third (the neutralizing or patterning) term comprises the relationship between the first and second terms which permits of the experience as such and constitutes a particular form of consciousness, namely a passively registering form.

From this analysis we may see, in the first place, that consciousness is not a thing but, instead, is a relationship, viz., that specific relationship which has just been defined above. And we may then ask: what degree of objective reality is possessed by I_O, the second term of the three-termed relationship whose third term is an actually passive form of consciousness? We recognize, since the relation of I_O to the source of its experience is a passive one, that the chief characteristic of I_O is passivity. This complete passivity may incline us at first to view I_O as a mere figment of the imagination, as something gratuitously invented to conform with a far-fetched theory. But that is not the case. Passivity is not synonomous with unreality. The reason that in this case we mistakenly assume it to be so synonomous, is that in this case we have an innate conviction that, if I is to exist at all, then the chief characteristic of I must be activity. Without arguing this last proposition we simply point out that, in the instance of I_O, the chief characteristic in fact present is complete passivity. But this does not signify that I_O is unreal; it means that I_O has the reality of an actual, though often unrecognized, postulation. And postulations are not necessarily imaginary or phantastic inventions; on the contrary, they often constitute the rationally required consequences of the nature of reality itself.

All this may give us a reasonably complete formulation of the situation as we now find it to exist in our own cases and in those of others; but the more interesting aspect of it lies in the surprising implications it furnishes of very curious possibilities. To put these implications as compactly as possible in our present terms: if an actually postulated I ($I_{\dot{o}}$), then potentially a pseudo-I ("I"); and if potentially a pseudo-I ("I"), then possibly a really genuine human I. The actualization of these possibilities, naturally, would be sequential rather than simultaneous.

What this comes down to practically, is the proposition: if $C_{\bar{p}}$, then potentially C_a. That is, if our consciousness is now demonstrably passive, then there exists at least the theoretical possibility that potentially it might become active.

However, if we are to proceed from I_O to I, we shall soon realize that it cannot be done directly; the progression must be from I_O to

"I" to I. The clue to the characteristics of "I" lies in the intermediate conditions necessary in order to transform C_p into C_a. These conditions require that the transformation, if possible at all, be a gradual one. And meantime "I", or I-in-quotation-marks, is not and cannot be a genuinely human I, with all the attributes of a genuinely human I. That is why we put it in quotation marks: to signify an approach toward, but not an identity with, a genuinely human I. In order to appreciate these points it will be well to contrast the attributes of the actual C_p with those of the potential C_a.

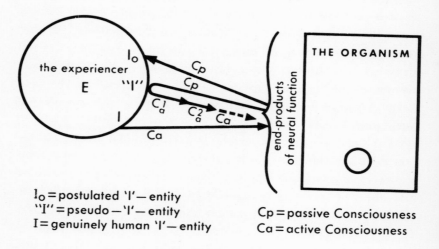

I_o = postulated 'I' — entity
"I" = pseudo — 'I' — entity
I = genuinely human 'I' — entity

C_p = passive Consciousness
C_a = active Consciousness

DIAGRAM II

Among the definitory attributes of C_p are these: that if the nerve impulse groups of the different stages 8, above, are sufficiently intense and especially if they include "pain"-impulses, then they force themselves upon the experiencer, I_o, that is, they create a relationship between O and I_o such that the latter cannot avoid some or other awareness of the experience. But if the mentioned qualifications are not met by the given nerve impulse groups, then no awareness of the occurrence takes place upon the part of I_O. Therefore we see that, with C_p obtaining, I_O is not only a purely passive registrant but an extremely inadequate one to boot. In other words, the subject is aware only of those events in his organism of which he cannot avoid awareness and, since avoidance is passively inevitable in the vast majority of cases, he is aware actually only of a tiny fraction of the constantly offered raw material of his own experience. To put it another way, the threshhold of passive consciousness might be said to be very high and only those few nerve impulse groups to succeed in crossing it which in themselves constitute an exceptional and very small minority among all the nerve impulse groups constantly present at the various stages 8 within the organism. From the direction of the organism this situation, being a purely mechanical one, cannot be altered.

But it is not really the threshhold of passive consciousness which is very high. This high threshhold actually pertains to the 'I'-entity, in the given instance to I_O; it no more pertains to the relationship called consciousness than it does to the organism, which is a purely mechanical contrivance serving nature in ways strictly predetermined by the design of its response-mechanisms. Similarly, the relationship obtaining between the 'I'-entity and the organism—which relationship constitutes the degree of consciousness prevailing in the given instance —is to be attributed properly to the degree of activity or of its lack manifested by the 'I'-entity itself. In the case of I_O the 'I'-entity, being entirely passive, necessarily exhibits an extremely passive relationship to the organism, viz., the relationship we have labelled C_p. The origin of this relationship (or degree of consciousness) is neither from the organism nor from the relationship itself; the origin is from I_O. For these reasons the high threshhold that prevents adequate experiential response to the raw neural material presented by the organism, is a threshhold of the 'I'-entity in its condition of I_O.

But is there any known characteristic of the 'I'-entity as such which dooms it inevitably to manifest as I_O? That it actually does so manifest in the cases which come under our observation, must be admitted, for *all* of the activity in these cases—and of course there is a great deal of it—should and must be attributed to the organism, leaving I_O as the non-active interpretor of neurological event into the quite different terms of subjective experience. For instance, I_O interprets a specific neural event in Brodmann's Area 17 as the subjective experience of color—let us say of the color, blue—which is certainly absent from that neural region. But it is absurd to suppose that I_O actively has invented the given experience, since it can be shown that no blueness is experienced in the absence of the specified neural event. This demonstration in itself shows the experience to be a *post facto* occurrence, as compared to the neurological one. And the same is as true of intellectual and emotional experience as of sensory experience.

But if we assert this to be the case, are we at the same time asserting that it is forever the necessary and unavoidable case? The writer can perceive no rational necessity that the second assertion must follow from the first; nor does he so assume. Surely it is possible theoretically that the 'I'-entity *might* manifest a greater degree of activity than it does under its guise as I_O. It is this possibility—that the 'I'-entity might manifest as "I" rather than as I_O—which we wish first to explore.

It is not necessary to premise any mystical incentives or any mystical stimuli precedent to such a change. If the possibility exist as a real one, then the adequate stimuli for its manifestation certainly could, and no doubt do, originate externally and are transmuted into the experience of the 'I'-entity through the mediation of the organism's receptor systems and the function of passive registration already manifested by I_O. There is no known characteristic of reality which denies that a passive I_O can entertain a suggestion from outside recommending an attempt to manifest more actively. If the suggestion should include any practicable means of doing so and if such a suggestion should be accepted, then immediately it will prove convenient to speak of "I" instead of I_O, to speak, that is, of an at least minimally active pseudo-I in place of the formerly completely passive I-postulation. That is simply because a real distinction has taken place and because our verbal labels should correspond with it.

What, then, is the nature of the activity in which the 'I'-entity as such can take part? It is definitely not mental, emotional or sensori-muscular, for these are exactly the fields already pre-empted by the experiential content originating from the neurological activity of the organism. In fact, any such suggestion misses the point entirely and simply shows that the nature of I_O has been misunderstood. It is the nature of I_O to experience passively and it does this by interpreting subjectively, *i.e.*, by registering passively the raw material of experience constantly being presented to it by the neural operations of the organism. The opposite of that situation is to register such data actively; but since this cannot be accomplished instantly or in a moment, the intermediate stage consists in an attempt upon the part of the 'I'-entity to take a more active attitude toward the end-products of the neural manifestation of the organism. And this attitude will include the attempt to lower the threshhold which, in the case of I_O, excludes so many otherwise potential neurological data from experience.

While such attempts are going forward and before they have been able fully to succeed, we speak of the involved 'I'-entity as "I" rather than as I_O because, although not as yet a fully genuine human I, it is presumably upon the way to becoming one and now bears a sufficient resemblance to justify the quotation marks instead of the sub-zero.

The limits of this chapter do not permit of a detailed description of the rigorous conditions which define a genuine activity upon the part of the 'I'-entity; but those conditions can be specified rigorously and shall be specified in such terms in the succeeding chapter. Meantime we may ask what the result would be of meeting those detailed conditions successfully. Certainly the result would be the eventual creation of a genuinely active human I; but in what ways would this genuine I differ from the I_0 of our currently universal acquaintance?

One respect that can hardly be doubted, would lie in the relationship between such an 'I'-entity and its associated organism, that is, in the type of consciousness then relating I to the organism rather than, as formerly, relating the organism to I_0. The type of consciousness then would be active instead of passive, which means, in effect, that the initiation of behavior then would inhere in the 'I'-entity rather than in the organism, because the preponderance of activity would be in I instead of in It.

Such an effect can be imagined by postulating a reversal of the sequence of behavior as now recognized. Our present sequence of behavior is as follows. First, some combination of external (or internal) stimuli causes the organism to respond in a given manner, that is, to behave. Second, not only the original stimuli but the immediately resulting behavior give rise to corresponding emotional sequences of experience in I_0. Third, in order to have some automatic explanation of this entirely mechanical train of events, the mental section of the organism's neural equipment supplies what (whether in mitigation of the response or not) is properly to be termed a rationalization of the whole performance. When this sometimes very active rationalization enters into I_0's passively registrant experience, two consequences follow, the first one false, the second one factual: 1) I_0 at once becomes convinced that he thought up the whole response; 2) one unit of our behavior sequences has been completed.

The reversal of such a sequence can be stated simply. First, the 'I'-entity—in this case a genuinely human I—comes to an intellectual decision, based upon correct reason, as to what his proposed behavior shall be. Second, such an active 'I'-entity experiences the normal (not the usual) emotion corresponding to the proposed behavior.

Third, the proposed behavior is carried into effect promptly and economically by the organism in question. All these three steps are mediated, as in the previously reversed case, by the neural equipment and later by the muscular equipment of the body; but the sequence is turned about because the initiation now comes from the 'I'-entity instead of, as before, from the organism. In the three-factored phenomenon which is a human being, the 'I'-entity has become the active factor and the organism the passive one, whereas the third or patterning factor, the element of consciousness, while maintaining its same orientation toward the whole, has altered from a passive to an active type of awareness. It is not to be thought, however, that such a total reversal of our long-ingrained behavior patterns can be achieved quickly or without the utmost effort.

Our natural hesitation to accept such a drastic possibility as a real potentiality of people like ourselves is a measure, not at all of the real impossibility of the accomplishment but, instead, only of the distance by which we honestly find ourselves severed from such an actuality. Certainly a genuinely human I, an active consciousness and the consequent paradic sequences of behavior are very far from being actual among us. It is not sought here to assert that any of these items is actual; it is sought only to show that a careful analysis of human consciousness presents them as real, not as imaginary or phantastic, potentialities.

chapter II

THE ACTIVATION
OF CONSCIOUSNESS

THE PROBLEM OF THE ACTIVATION of the human consciousness is
one whose difficulty and sublety cannot be overemphasized. Especially
is this so in the case of the naturally predisposed intellectualist or
'thinker,' for he is that type of man in whom the cortical activity of
the correlation neurones is very complex and frequently very intense
also. This intensity, registered in his actually passive experience, makes
it most difficult for him to recognize that the activity is not his own
but, instead, is that of his nervous system.

To be sure, the purpose implied here is to make the activity his
own eventually; but obviously, if he mistakenly assumes that it is
now already his own, nothing can be accomplished toward reversing
his really passive consciousness until his mistaken opinion about its
present nature has been reversed. A great many persons entertain
the false belief that their consciousness is active when in fact all of
the involved activity is simply neurological. One way in which to
destroy the delusion is through careful and sincere reflection upon
the true nature of the case; the other is by means of the technique
shortly to be described, through the practice of which anyone may

become convinced that his behavior is mechanical and automatic, including his mental behavior.

Thus the first great difficulty is the false assumption that, because the thoughts are active, therefore the consciousness or conscious-relation-to-them is active. If this does not arise from the mistaken identification of consciousness with thought process, it will often lead to it. But consciousness is no more to be identified with thought process (despite the latter's complexity) than with the knee jerk, or any other purely physiological, reflex. Thought process, too, is neurological activity, but consciousness is the relationship to neurological activity which creates experience for the subject. And since this situation is supposed somehow to be derogatory of the intellectualist, there is an added difficulty to be overcome.

But if we realize that consciousness is to be distinguished equally from physical movement, from sensory response, from basal gangliar response *and* from the frontal lobe responses of the correlation centers, then we reach the real subtlety of the problem. For we ask: what else is there in addition to those four kinds of responses? What can a man do which is neither movement nor sensing nor emotional feeling nor intellection? Some say that this was the original riddle of the Sphinx; but whether or not they are right on that score, it is still a subtle riddle.

It is subtle because our first answers all involve, upon examination, some form of sensing or of feeling or of thinking and by definition these must be incorrect answers, since all such activities must be excluded by the form of the question itself. Nevertheless, there does exist a legitimate solution. And it is so simple that almost everyone immediately rejects it either as meaningless or as incredible.

The novel, and indeed the sole, activity in which the subject himself can engage purely upon his own initiative is an active *awareness* of all of the aforementioned processes.

This may sound easy but it is indeed an extremely formidable undertaking even to understand the exact meaning of such a type of awareness. Our usual awareness is an automatic response to predetermined stimulation and it is precisely this type of awareness that is passive in character and that defines our passive type of consciousness. What is indicated now is an *active* type of awareness; and the reversed distinction is highly difficult to apprehend.

Of what is one to be aware in this fashion? There is only a single entity of which one can be aware directly, and that is one's own body. Our previous analysis has shown that its neurological phenomena constitute the direct points of contact between the subject and his organism but our first attempt will demonstrate conclusively that we are simply unable to be conscious directly of those billions of complex neural happenings. In the case of one who asserts such an ability, we rightly judge him to be dealing in phantasy. But there is something still closer to us than the neurological phenomena themselves; and that is the experiences to which they give rise. Furthermore, there is a way in which we can be aware actively not only of the experiences but of what the experiences mean. That way, however, cannot involve introspection, for introspection is not awareness; it is a thought process of which, like others, we become passively aware only later.

Let us point to our muscular tensions, and specifically to those of our facial muscles. Ordinarily we never notice them but that is far from saying that we are prohibited from noticing them, for in fact we can do so at this very moment if we wish. The tensions in our cheeks and forehead, the tensions about our lips and those around our jaws, all of them are there to be noticed if we wish to be aware of them. Moreover, we can be aware of their combinations, the integrations of these tensions which in themselves constitute our facial expressions of the moment. Other people notice our expressions clearly (and react objectively to them); it is only we ourselves who habitually and lazily disregard them, remaining unaware of what our expressions are saying both to others and to ourselves. This, then, is one category of our bodies' behavior of which we can be conscious actively if we decide to do so. Doing so, we shall at once realize, if only through the effort expended, that such an awareness is a consciously active one.

Although they are not infinite in number, there are other categories of our gross behavior which can be treated in the same way as the muscular tensions that comprise our facial expressions. These are: posture, or the static positions our bodies assume from time to time; gesture, or the part-movements that occur frequently and that are characteristic of the individual organism, such as local movements of the shoulders, arms and hands, of the legs and head; movement, or the general motion of the body as a whole, as in walking, running, playing tennis or golf, and so on; tone of voice, or the intonation that accompanies our words and by which others judge of their meaning more accurately than by the literal significance of the words themselves. As to all these five categories of our gross behavior it is possible for us to be aware of them actively when they occur, to a far greater extent than we ever are aware of them.

Manifestly such awareness of our physical behaviors must take place concurrently with their happening, since otherwise what is activated will be memory; and memory is not consciousness but a thought process, mediated by certain of the neurological phenomena of the cortex. This primary distinction between consciousness and thought process must be kept in mind always during the discussion, for consciousness is a relationship, the difference between its passive and active aspects being the difference between our customary scarcely conscious registration of our bodies' behavior and our active observation of the same.

This concurrence of awareness with the events of which we may be aware, likewise presents the reply to the frequent objection that, if we are to spend our time being conscious actively of all these bodily phenomena, we shall have no time for anything else. But if awareness be concurrent with the phenomena observed, then quite literally *it takes no time,* since it happens simultaneously with the organic behaviors that are its objects. What is indicated, is a *new* activity on the part of the subject (I_0), a subjective activity accompanying the objective organic activities already in progress. Since these two kinds of activity coincide temporally, no extra temporal duration can be involved.

Let us now consider the means by which the above type of awareness can take place. In the case of our gross bodily behavior these means are our sensations, usually unconsciously registered but consciously observable potentially. With regard to facial expression our awareness is mediated by sensations of muscular tension, with regard to posture by tensions, pressures and the sense of equilibrium. These three sensations, together with kinaesthetic sensations from tendons and joints, are also the chief mediators in the instances of gesture and movement. As to tone of voice, the mediation naturally is through audition or the sense of hearing. In some cases the visual sense also can become a collateral mediator. The point is that observations of this character are made by means of our sensations.

A further point is this: that the raw sensations themselves can become the objects of an active awareness to a degree far beyond our usual experience. Take for example the field of vision: habitually only the focus of sight is clear to us, and that only partially, while we miss almost all of the periphery. But by an effort of attention it is possible to be aware of much more of the field than usual, even when our eyes are focussed for reading. This involves more kinds of attention than one but we shall see that by active subjective effort the span of attention can be increased greatly. Activity of such a nature is also part of an active consciousness.

The categories of sensation are generally agreed upon and may be listed as follows:

vision (sight)
audition (hearing)
gustation (taste)
olfaction (smell)
pain
equilibrium
pressure: deep
      light
      tickle
temperature: heat
        cold
kinaesthetic: movement

So far we have been concerned with the objects toward which the 'I'-entity can manifest an active attention and of which it can become aware directly in an active rather than a passive sense. All of these objects consist of the phenomena presented by the organism with which the particular 'I'-entity is associated, and they comprise not only the gross physical behaviors of posture, gesture, movement, facial expression and tone of voice but also the various sensations originating from the sensory equipment of the organism. But the 'I'-entity in its present guise of I_0 is both immature from the standpoint of a genuinely human I and in addition its customary state is that condition of lightly hypnotized trance which we call the Waking state. It is on account of these contemporary infirmities that, in the first attempt to transform I_0 into "I" or the transitional condition of pseudo-I, the earliest objects of active awareness must be both simple and gross.

These are the first toddling exercises of an infant 'I'-entity, for it is obvious that toddling must come before walking, just as walking must come before running and acrobatics. To be aware actively for any length of time of any one of the above categories is at first an impossible feat for I_O and, when it is stated that one of the criteria of "I" is the ability to be aware actively of all of them simultaneously, some measure of the difficulty of the transformation can be appreciated.

These difficulties are enhanced when we come to a description of the *way* in which such active awareness must be manifested. The reader may suppose that awareness is a simple matter, an irreducible factor in the situation. But this sort of awareness is far from that; it is a specifically defined activity and, as such, it must be described in rigorously specific terms. Comparable descriptions have been made in the past in numerous languages and under many forms of expression but here we wish to employ a scientific formulation. From that point of view there are seven defining characteristics of the technique of active awareness. It will be best to discuss these briefly *seriatim*.

The first defining characteristic of awareness is the total absence from it of any element of criticism, either positive or negative. In other words, the lack either of disapprobation or of approbation as to what is being observed. It is plain that no scientist in his laboratory could make proper observations of a hitherto unknown creature if concurrently he were to be lost in admiration of this excellent worm or if, alternatively, he were to be concerned with disapproving judgments of the miserable animal. He looks to see, not to judge; and awareness is awareness, it is not judgment. Certainly it is not criticism, pro or con.

The second defining characteristic is that active awareness excludes tutorialness. For if criticism is out of place, any attempt to alter what is observed must be even more so, or even any consideration of such an attempt. To observe is to observe, it is not to seek to improve; and in fact any change whatever must deprive us at once of the primary object of observation. Tutorialness is comparable to the back-effects of instrumentation upon a laboratory subject, which often invalidate the entire experiment. If we are observing the habits of armadillos, we do not seek to make them either more or less neighborly than is their nature, else we shall fail in our purpose of finding out what actually they are like.

The third characteristic is the absence from active awareness of any element of mental or logical analysis. This prohibition must follow from the sharp and final distinction between consciousness and thought process. To be aware is not to be thinking; thinking has its place in life but not in awareness. Analysis is a mental process and as such it must be excluded from pure awareness.

The absence of analytical accompaniment from the act of awareness means that one must not be thinking about the object of awareness but, instead, must be observing it solely. And this same characteristic of the technique answers another objection often raised, namely, that to have one's attention taken up in this way will inevitably mean that we shall become so concerned with our behavior as to be unconscious of our surroundings and even to risk possible injury from them. That indeed would be true if we were to become engrossed in thinking about (or even in remembering) the behaviors we observe and thus have all our attention concentrated upon them. But the attention required for awareness is a different kind of attention from that involved in thinking or in the mental following of trains of cause and effect, and so on. The actual effect of active awareness, correctly manifested, is and must be to increase both the accuracy and the speed of our cognizance of the external environment, because the latter depends upon the activity of our receptor mechanisms which has now been increased by our active consciousness of their products. While crossing the street, we are far less likely to be struck down if concurrently we are observing ourselves in the prescribed manner than if we are lost, as is often the case, in phantastic daydreams or in resentment over some fancied slight. But this result is to be obtained only if (among other characteristics) all thought process be excluded from this kind of awareness.

The objection mentioned above has a meaning only when the prohibition of thinking is disregarded. Thinking about the objects of awareness indeed will interfere with other thought processes occurring simultaneously. But if awareness be held strictly to a *purely* conscious activity, it will not and cannot interfere with any other activities concurrently taking place in the organism. To the contrary, it will sharpen and increasingly activitate them in turn.

With the fourth characteristic we come to one of the outstanding subtleties of the entire subject and the reader is warned that it is more difficult to grasp than it appears. Ordinarily we are fully identified with our physical organisms. We say: I *am* Thomas J. Jones or C. Daly King, or whatever the name by which the given organism may be called. Indeed, this identification with the organism is one of the defining characteristics of the I_O condition of the 'I'-entity and one of the main features of the trance state in which it exists.

For the purposes of active awareness such an attitude toward the organism must be completely reversed; and what is required specifically is *non*-identification from the organism. For the usual statement, I am a body, there must be substituted the assertion, I *have* a body, and a full distinction must be made between I and It.

In view of our long-established tender consideration for all aspects of our bodily manifestations this is by no means an easy attitude to take toward the named organism but, when exercising active awareness toward it, this must be done explicitly and without equivocation. The first step is to set up clearly in one's thought processes the concept of the I and the It as contrasted entities and thus for the 'I'-entity to take up a position of non-identification from the organism.

But that is only a preliminary step and must not be confused with the awareness to follow. At the original Institute of Gurdjieff this preliminary was called self-remembering and the distinction between it and the later awareness was recognized fully. It sometimes happened later, however, when the sequence was not sufficiently emphasized, that certain pupils became confused about this sequential distinction and eventually fell into the error of equating the preliminary concept of non-identification or self-remembering (a thought process) with the act of awareness itself. Non-identification is an essential condition of genuine awareness but it is not in itself the act of which it is a precedent condition. When only self-remembering or non-identification from the organism has taken place, the act of awareness has not yet occurred. That is a relatively easy mistake to make and its erroneous nature must be insisted upon here.

Only after the contrast between I and It is fully clear and present, does one observe the manifestations of the body from a completely non-identified point of view. Such manifestations are to be observed not as those of oneself but as if they were those of someone else altogether. When one observes the behaviors of one's organism, it must be at a stranger that one is looking. In this way, and only in this way, is it possible to acquire and to maintain that impartiality which is an essential characteristic of active awareness.

If there be any identification whatever with the object of active awareness, then the awareness is colored necessarily not only by the criticism, tutorialness and analysis aforesaid but by all sorts of further subjective engulfments. And, in addition, the 'I'-entity at once loses its objectivity and subsides immediately into its previous state of mere postulation and passive registration. It is a condition of I_0 that it exists as a necessary postulation; it is an equally defining condition of "I" that it exist at least as the conception of an objective entity. That which observes is not that which is observed, for there can be no observation in the absence of a distinct observer. An accurate and literal non-identification from the organism is precisely what permits an active awareness of the manifestations of the organism to take place.

The fifth defining characteristic of active awareness is that it shall be confined to the prescribed area of the manifestations of the organism. By no means everything can be the object of a legitimate active awareness. Such an awareness is a direct awareness and thus nothing external to the body can be one of its objects, since all externality is represented indirectly through the body's own receptor mechanisms. And likewise, for reasons of prematurity, very many of the phenomena of the organism are unsuitable or impossible for observation by the immature 'I'-entity. The legitimate objects of active awareness have already been listed as the mentioned categories of gross physical behavior and as those of the given sensations.

The sixth defining characteristic consists in the use of all appropriate mediations in the process of active awareness. In the cases of the categories of gross behavior a single sensation will seldom suffice to construct the bodily image which is to be the object of non-identified awareness. In some instances more sensations will be available than in others but in every instance all sensations appropriate to the full reporting of the given manifestation should be utilized in the observation of it.

The seventh characteristic is that the exercise of active awareness cannot be confined to any special time or place. It is not, like Swedish exercises, to be practiced for fifteen minutes each morning in one's bedroom nor is it comparable to the petitional prayers uttered by the devout at night before retiring. Active awareness is related to the establishment of a state of consciousness at least as different from Waking as Waking is from Sleep and, since states of consciousness endure over relatively long time-periods, no specially confined period of time is appropriate for the exercise of active awareness. One goal of the technique is the establishment of a more active state of consciousness—and with it a more objective 'I'-entity—not for some given period of the day but at any time, at will. Since it is a condition of a particular state of consciousness, it must endure as long as that conscious state lasts. And if one desires the conscious state to become a permanent attribute, then there can be no temporal restriction of the activity that alone can make it so.

We may summarize the characteristics of active awareness as:

1) excluding any element of criticism;

2) excluding any element of tutorialness;

3) excluding any element of analysis or other mental process;

4) involving a complete non-identification from the organism;

5) being directed only toward the prescribed area of objectivity;

6) involving the mediation of all sensations appropriate to its objects;

7) not being limited in its exercise to any special times or places.

The core of this technique and by far its most important feature lies in its fourth definitory characteristic, the attitude of non-identification from which it is exercised. This objectivizing of the 'I'-entity by setting it to one side while the organic body is set to another side, involves in the first place a distinct division of our energies of attention; and it implies the eventual effect of rendering the 'I'-entity real in an objective rather than the postulational sense in which it is real under presently ordinary conditions.

It implies also the possibility of a state of consciousness beyond our ordinary present experience, of greater clarity and extent than the Waking state to which we are accustomed but having no relation whatever with so-called mystical experiences and being in fact almost the opposite of the latter with their confusions and inarticulateness. Yet although non-identification is the most important feature of active awareness, it is not the only one and all seven defining characteristics, as rigorously described above, must be present without fail if active awareness is to be exercised. If a single characteristic be lacking, then, whatever may be taking place, it cannot, by definition, be active awareness.

This particular technique is not at all a new invention or a new discovery in the annals of psychology, although its definition as above may be of fairly recent formulation. The earliest of the ancient Egyptians knew it as Scrutiny or the technique of the Eye of Hur; indeed it is related to the caption of their ancient Ritual Chapters, now miscalled the *Book of the Dead* but whose actual title is *Peret-em-heru,* the *Achievement of Consciousness.* The Gnostics, before they became mystical and superstitious, knew it under a name that has been translated as Light-Gaining. At the Gurdjieff Institute it went under the title of Self-Observation, a somewhat confusing terminology, since what is observed is not at all the self—the 'I'-entity can never observe the 'I'-entity. Instead, it is the phenomena of the associated physical organism that are the objects of the directed awareness. But whatever the names and in whatever terms the activity be described, it is always the same activity: an active awareness of organic phenomena and the related establishment of the observing 'I'-entity as an objective reality.

It is sometimes objected that the suggested theoretical technique is too difficult and far too uncustomary to be effective, if practically applied. But even without attempting to explain in other terms the accomplishments of those who have practiced this technique—the accomplishments of the ancient Egyptians, for example, with their amazing astronomical knowledge in the absence of any modern instrumentation and with their equally amazing architectural and constructional abilities in the case of the so-called Great Pyramid—there is a simpler and more common sense reply to the protest. Since the writer himself has undergone this discipline and since he has instructed others in it and has tested the effects in his own and other cases by properly objective methods, he knows that those effects are neither confined to himself nor do they constitute some subjective delusion upon his part. They are fully objective and confirmable by any competent worker in psychology who has investigated the process.

It is necessary to emphasize here, however, that the difficulty and the unquestionable practical effects of the technique of active aware-ness, as defined, make this discipline a very dangerous one in the absence of continual, adequate and competent supervision while it is being practiced. The pitfalls both of misunderstanding and of resulting mistaken practice cannot be exaggerated. It is not for the light-hearted, amateur experimenter; and because of the very real results that must follow inevitably upon either its correct or its incorrect application, the hazards to be encountered are of a much more drastic sort than arise in the case of mere theoretical speculation. In certain cases the most deplorable consequences have occurred and always they have been traceable directly to errors which, though seemingly slight, have produced very injurious effects. Experience shows that, apart from the great difficulty of understanding the technique in its correct formulation, most persons simply are not sufficiently sceptical to practice it in the absence of the strictest supervision by a competent instructor who has already preceded them along this road.

A qualified and effective organization is also a *sine qua non* of the technique, only within which its discipline can be undergone safely. There are too many aspects of the technique which cannot be explained adequately in a one-sided or non-Socratic discussion. The reader is warned in the most serious terms not to experiment with this method upon his own responsibility.

Yet that in this technique there exists a practicable means for the activation of the human consciousness—and for the transformation of the postulated I_0 at least into the partially objective "I" or pseudo-I

—can scarcely be doubted by an impartial inquirer willing to spend the time and effort necessary to examine the matter. However, this is not a book of advocacy but of exposition. Its subject is the nature of human consciousness and we must now proceed to a description of the various states in which that consciousness is to be experienced actually and potentially.

chapter III

THE STATES
OF CONSCIOUSNESS

THE FULL SPAN of the states of consciousness said to be accessible
to human beings, comprises the following four: Sleep, Waking,
Awakeness, Objective Consciousness.

Alternative names that have been given to the third and fourth
states respectively, are Self-Consciousness and Cosmic Consciousness.
However called, they are, of course, the same states or conditions of
the conscious entity. But Self-Consciousness has frequently, though
incorrectly, been used to refer to the ordinary Waking state and thus
a less ambiguous term is preferable for the third state of consciousness,
which is to be distinguished sharply from ordinary Waking. And we
prefer to reserve the term, Cosmic Consciousness, for the abnormal
variety of Objective Consciousness that is experienced pathologically
by so-called mystics. Therefore in our discussion we shall adhere to
the four terms first stated above, with the understanding that both
Awakeness and Objective Consciousness are considered as normal
or paradic states of consciousness implicit in the design of the human
being.

In this chapter we shall have to consider seriously just what is
meant by the nowadays uncertain term, normal. Due to the widespread use of the words, normal and norm, in a mathematical, and

especially a statistical, sense, they have lost much of their originally accurate meanings and have come to signify average, mean, median or modal, and also what is typical of a given class of measures or entities. Under certain conditions it is thus possible to call the abnormal the norm and it is often done, to the destruction of any objective meaning at all. Properly speaking, the normal is that which functions healthily, properly and correctly, not that which is, or may be, typical of malfunctioning entities. Because of these misuses we propose here to employ the term, paradic (from paradigm), in order to indicate that which functions in accordance with its inherent design; and this word, paradic, will be used hereafter in place of the inaccurate adjective, normal, and the confusing noun or substantive, norm. The term, abnormal, however, still is used in its correct connotations of distorted, diseased, or in some degree unhealthy or unfitted. We shall employ abnormal in this way.

We are reasonably well acquainted with the two states or degrees of consciousness between which all of us are accustomed to alternate daily and which are generally called Sleep and Waking. Our data concerning the former state are voluminous, including metabolic and generally physiological measurements, AC electrical measurements (as in brain wave or electroencephalographic phenomena) and DC electrical measurements (testifying to the basic alteration of the biological field in Sleep), as well as data on gross movements and even subjective oral reports, not very reliable, of subjective experience in dream.

The objective data are in remarkable agreement, considering the diverse regions from which they originate. They demonstrate a quiescent physical condition, with many of the organic functions slowing to a much diminished tempo and a metabolic condition dedicated to the elaboration of organic energies for current, but mainly for future, use. In fact we know so many details relevant to the state of Sleep that the next chapter will be devoted to them.

The generic design of Sleep, its inherent structure as it were, is very simple and also quite obvious. It consists in the retardation of those processes that are most active in the Waking state, in the realignment of the focus of organic activity from the periphery to the interior of the body and in the detachment of the experiencer, the 'I'-entity, from the end-products of organic neural function. Thus consciousness of any kind is reduced more and more until, finally, experience ceases and the experiencer rests completely. In this optimum Sleep state the striped musculature of the organism is fully relaxed and, although the receptors still respond to external stimulation, their connections with the arrival platforms of the cortex are interrupted neurologically. To most intents and purposes the relation of the human being to the outside world is broken.

That is the design of Sleep and that is its general description as a normal or paradic process. But clearly it is not what we ourselves enjoy nor what our carefully observed subjects enjoy. Our kind of Sleep is as plain and abnormal a violation of the above principles as the principles themselves are plain and paradic.

We toss and turn, we moan and snore and, if there be an interval of seeming quiet with a gentle and even breathing rate, investigators using the subjective techniques of psychoanalysis and similar methods always have maintained that waking the subject at such a moment discloses a rich and varied content of subjective dream experience. However, a recent research suggests that only about 20 per cent of the Sleep period is filled with such dream content. (1). That this content is divorced from the logical sequences of external reality, is reasonable enough when we consider the neural condition of the organism, with its sensory arrival platforms severed neurologically from the receptors. But the dream experiences constantly maintain muscular tensions contradictory to the organic paradic of Sleep; and certainly few, if any, of our dreams are restful or recuperative in kind. Predictably from the organic design of Sleep we should not dream at all. Our Sleep is abnormal because neither we nor our organisms obtain from it the designed amounts of rest.

In great part this results from the abnormality of our Waking experience, which is defined by our present inadequately and passively registering type of consciousness. Previous analysis has shown that the Waking state also is characterized by a reversed functional condition in which first we receive unforeseen external stimulation, then react automatically to it both emotionally and by mechanical physical response, and finally rationalize the preceding process in order to have some explanation of it. But the rationalization is largely irrational; this is obvious to mere inspection and even the political pollsters now have reached the conclusion that there is "growing evidence that the voters could not be depended upon to be rational." (2). As one instance of their irrationality, their image of the perfect President is cited as that of one having "great warmth, inspiring confidence rather than admiration and being not so proper that he is unbelievable. He must have a sense of humor. His stand on individual political issues"—the only legitimately rational item on the list —"is relatively unimportant". (3).

The Waking state is characterized also by a certain degree of hypnosis, both externally and internally induced. A leading feature of the hypnotic state is suggestibility of the subject, seen not only in political opinions but plainly in the effects produced by advertising, wherein mere repetition suffices to establish absurd beliefs, such as big-equals-best. In the matter of value-standards the same suggestibility is encountered and indeed is the origin of phaulophilia among us. This inclination to accept and to believe everything one hears or reads, however absurd, "authoritative," or merely journalistic, has become now so thoroughly established that it demonstrates clearly the hypnotic degree of the Waking state, in which the ability to judge for oneself and from one's own experience has been lost almost wholly.

Another characteristic of the Waking state, perhaps no more

abnormal than the preceding but even more important, is that in this state of consciousness the three chief human functions—mental, emotional and practical—never are exercised equally. The energies requisite to their activities are elaborated within the organism by its metabolic processes but these energies are drawn upon haphazardly and the upshot is that the subject comes to the end of the day with too much energy remaining in the reservoirs and with this surplus distributed unevenly. These surplus energies spill over and supply the impetus for nocturnal dreams, with the effect of disturbing the paradic restfulness of Sleep. In other words, it is the abnormality of the Waking state which is the direct cause of the abnormality of Sleep.

The third and fourth states of consciousness ordinarily are not experienced and for us they remain only as unfulfilled potentialities. Many people experience infrequent flashes of them but, when these occur without forewarning or intent (as they do), they constitute poor evidence even for the reality of such states.

The third state here is called Awakeness. It is characterized by an active instead of a passive consciousness, in it the 'I'-entity is in active observation of the associated organism and it is this type of consciousness that serves as a kind of governor for the three chief functions, regulating them harmoniously and thus expending their natural energies in a balanced flow. It will be seen that this third state of consciousness is simply the paradic counterpart of the abnormal Waking state as ordinarily experienced; it is featured by a complete reversal of the consciousness-relationship from passivity to activity and in it a paradic sequence of behavior is established for the first time: precedently thought, secondly emotion, finally action. When present, it usurps the place of the abnormal Waking state and permits of paradic Sleep when the time for the latter is due.

The fourth state is Objective Consciousness and the paradic way to it is through and from Awakeness to Objective Consciousness. In the state of Objective Consciousness the relation of the subject to cosmic phenomena (the genuine physics and chemistry of the Universe, for example, and the real nature of sidereal phenomena) is the same as is his relation to his own organism in Awakeness. He is aware of such events actively, directly and correctly, not as at present through the media of questionable mental constructs and hypothetical abstractions. Since this state, though definitely implied by the paradic design of the human being, never is experienced by us its characteristics now exist only as rational postulates and the state itself becomes a matter for discussion rather than assertion.

This state cannot be entered directly or correctly from the Waking state and, if it is entered from the Waking State, we find the abnormal variety of Objective Consciousness, often called Cosmic Consciousness and quite falsely esteemed as a boon.

A number of the features of Cosmic Consciousness clearly demonstrate its abnormality, when entered from the Waking state: it occurs suddenly and involuntarily; it produces flashes of so-called illumination, the details of which, however, are not subject to normal recall, either recent or distant; it departs as abruptly as it came, also involuntarily, and thus it cannot either be entered or be left at will; the experiences undergone while in it ordinarily cannot be described later in a way intelligible to the subject himself, let alone to anyone else, and thus they are quite unconfirmable, since they cannot even be stated accurately. All these characteristics of Cosmic Consciousness, as reported by its victims, are manifestly abnormal; indeed they clearly resemble those of a pathological condition and equally plainly are due to the immaturity of the subject, I_O.

Consequently we see that the abnormality of the Waking state induces a corresponding abnormality in the states both below and above it, Sleep and Objective Consciousness. Were abnormal Waking to be transformed into its paradic counterpart of Awakeness, the above would no longer be the case and the normal or paradic counterpart of Cosmic Consciousness, which is Objective Consciousness, would then become a real possibility. Objective Consciousness can be entered at will and properly only from an already established state of Awakeness, after the experiencer of the latter, the 'I'-entity at its own degree of "I", has achieved the further maturity that permits it to be named as a genuinely human I.

To summarize, we experience at present two abnormal states of consciousness, abnormal Sleep and Waking. But we may well possess the potentialities required for experiencing the full range of paradic conscious states: paradic Sleep, Awakeness and Objective Consciousness. The normal or paradic progression for human beings is from the first of the latter through the second to the third. And for ordinary men the key to all these genuinely normal states lies in the possibility of transforming the present abnormal Waking state into a potentially normal Awakeness, which is at the same time a step toward the ultimate maturity and normality of the now undeveloped 'I'-entity.

REFERENCES IN THE TEXT OF CHAPTER III

1) Dement, W. The effect of dream deprivation. *Science,* 10 June, 1960, 131: 1705-1707.
2) Packard, V. *The hidden persuaders.* D. McKay Co., N.Y., 1957, p. 184..
3) Packard, V. *Ibid.,* p. 186

chapter IV

SLEEP

THE FIRST OF THE GENERAL STATES of consciousness to be considered is that of Sleep. Like the other basic states a prime characteristic of Sleep is that it constitutes a general condition not only of the whole human organism but of the human subject himself as such. Indeed this is the fundamental definition of all the distinguishable states of consciousness: that they do not comprise part-reactions affecting mere subdivisions of the economy but, instead, that they involve the entire human entity, placing it *as a whole* in specified conditions of which the four selected terms serve as verbal labels.

This, of course, does not prejudice the further fact that it is possible to distinguish various different levels of Sleep, each with its characteristic minor symptoms whereby it can be discriminated from its counterparts. That is also the case with regard to the Waking state and possibly likewise in respect of the two further potential states of consciousness as well. But it does not alter the circumstance that all four are general conditions which encompass all the subordinate portions of the integrated or partially integrated organism.

In addition to these points it must be noted that there are also certain partial conditions such as hibernation, narcosis and anaesthesia, which may result from the administration of various drugs or poisons that produce insensibility and either motor or sensory paralysis. Here some, but not all, of the symptoms of genuine Sleep may appear. They are brought about often deliberately and always from external sources and their effects are usually chiefly upon some subdivision of the entire economy, as may be seen in the instance of local anaesthesia with its paralytic effect upon the sensory function of specific pain end-organs. With such partial conditions as these we shall not be concerned when treating of the general state of Sleep.

A good preliminary definition of Sleep is that it is the biological necessity for rest recurring periodically in the absence of special stimuli imposed from outside.

A large amount of work has been done upon the physiological symptoms or criteria by which the Sleep state is described and we may look first at these findings in order to have a comprehensive picture of the organic condition. The more important findings that have been reported, are summarized under the headings below:

skeletal musculature and position—

closure of eyelids;

outward divergence of eyeballs;

pupillary constriction, such that during Sleep all influences except accommodation and the light reflex widen the pupil;

usual absence of righting reflexes;

incomplete relaxation of skeletal musculature;

individual differences in bodily positions assumed;

relaxation of abdominal wall;

diminution of action potentials;

less relaxation on the part of infants than of adults (this last finding is very questionable).

reflexes—

    decrease in reinforcement from higher centers;

    knee jerk diminished or absent;

    cutaneous reflexes weakened or absent;

    preservation of the pupillary reflex;

    preservation of reflexes affecting heart rate, blood pressure, vasomotor and respiratory activity;

    abolishment of vestibular reflexes;

    reinstatement of a positive Babinski, evidencing a nervous system functional depression;

    absence of evidence of spinal cord sleep (Tarchanov).

digestion—

    unaffected;

    gastric and intestinal motility and the secretion of bile also unaffected.

heat production—

    decrease of basal heat production.

body temperature—

    decreased;

    possible causes conjectured to be muscular relaxation, horizontal vasomotor adjustments and a diurnal sleep-waking curve;

    fall in hypothalamic temperature greater than that in cortical temperature (Serota).

kidneys—

    decrease in excretion of chlorides and phosphates;

    decrease in water excretion parallel with that in temperature.

hypophysis and adrenals—

no good evidence of alteration in function or composition.

blood—

no retreat of calcium from blood to brain;

pH slightly lower, increased acidity;

rise in blood sugar, due to increased acidity;

cholesterol decrease;

vasoconstriction;

increase in blood volume, a possible cause being posture, producing a fluid return to blood vessels due to increased filtration pressure and increasing plasma volume, although the red cell count is lowered;

last mentioned cause is probably responsible for all, or nearly all, blood alterations.

heart—

decrease in heart rate;

large individual variations in heart rate;

probable causes are low metabolism, muscular relaxation, lowered reflex excitability, higher vagal tonus and parasympathetic dominance.

circulation—

decrease in blood pressure, systolic being more affected than diastolic;

exceptional high blood pressures, resulting from nightmares, may be so severe as to cause hemorrhage;

no cranial volume increase in blood but rather a cranial expansion with increased pressure and volume.

respiration —

> alterations chiefly due to position;

> evidence of thoracic breathing while asleep vs. abdominal breathing while awake;

> individual differences in rate, some showing increase, others decrease;

> increased irregularity during drowsiness, increased regularity during sleep, and occasional Cheyne-Stokes breathing when falling asleep;

> much individual variation; increased regularity (Kleitman), a Cheyne-Stokes tendency (Jenness);

> Cheyne-Stokes polypnea yielding a negative Babinski, apnea yielding a positive Babinski (Tournay);

> increase in depth of respiration (Mendicini);

> decrease in O_2 intake, with greater decrease in CO_2 output;

> lower respiratory quotient caused by muscular relaxation;

> increased CO_2 partial pressure in alveolar air, increased CO_2 tension in blood, slightly increased blood pH, thus lower respiratory center irritability may be a *result* of sleep.

electrical skin resistance —

> general rise in resistance, said to be due to decrease in mental activity affecting sweat gland activity.

cerebrum —

> sleep not abolished by decortication of dogs, monkeys and babies; abolishment of twenty-four hour cycle by decortication.

E.E.G.—

waves decrease (Berger) or disappear (Adrian and Yama-giwa);

stages according to Davis, Davis, Loomis, Harvey and Hobart:

A. interrupted alpha (or beta)

B. 'floating'; waves smooth with small, intermittent undulations

C. definite sleep; spindles (14-15/sec.) or some delta with spindles superposed

D. spindles plus random (very slow delta)

E. random, very slow delta;

stages according to Blake and Gerard:

1. awake; alpha (about 10/sec.)

2. light sleep; alpha plus delta (stages A, B, C, above)

3. deep sleep; delta, no alpha (stage D, above)

4. very light end-sleep; intermittant alpha

5. awake again; alpha;

sleep halves shown not to be mirror-images, lighter sleep in second half of period;

occurrence of many movements without change in sleep level (Loomis, Harvey and Hobart);

occurrence of changes in sleep level without movement (Loomis, Harvey and Hobart);

after movement, any change in level usually upward;

no continuous sleep curve;

brain waves altered by temperature, drugs, illness;

occurrence in cat of different wave forms for waking, for sleep or barbiturates and for ether anaesthesia (Bremer);

alternating sleep and wakefulness on cephalic side of lower
medullar section in cat;

deep sleep in cat with section behind N. III; cutaneous and
proprioceptive influences absent, although olfactory and
visual remain.

It will be recalled that the steady-state DC field of the organism
constitutes the third or patterning factor of the biological entity.
This is shown, in part, by the fact that this field is measurable by
means of its potential differences in the egg and embryo long before
any structural differentiation has taken place and that the later
neuraxis of the developed organism always lies along the line of the
greatest embryonic potential difference. (3). Since the organic field
bears so close (and apparently determining) a relationship to the
eventual creature's structural form, (4), it is to be supposed that its
relationship to function may also be a close one, especially to such
general functional aspects as those of the Sleep and Waking states.
In humans this question has been investigated with the following
results.

DC field alterations during sleep—

decrease in the mean values of the potential differences
within all three chief subdivisions of the nervous system
respectively;

gradual reduction of the characteristic waking differences
in electromotive force which distinguish one individual
from another at a given time and from himself at other
times;

less intersubject variability with regard to the three chief
sub-divisions of the nervous system;

less variability among the potential differences of the three
chief subdivisions of the nervous system;

what this means, in a graph, is that the Waking chart, full of
notches and zigzags representative of moment-to-moment
changes in the field, becomes an almost straight line
during Sleep;

all of the above alterations are so great as to be "significant"
in the accepted scientific sense.

The above summary of conditions during the Sleep state has been
abstracted chiefly from Kleitman's treatment of the subject, (12),
the last portion on DC field alterations from the work of the writer.
(11). This is by no means a full statement of all the physiological
evidence available nor even a complete summary of all the work that
has been done but it will give a good idea of the organic conditions
accompanying the Sleep state. When we ask, however, whether these
conditions are the symptoms or the definitions of Sleep and whether
they may be considered as its causes or its effects, the answer must be
that they are symptoms, not definitions, and that they comprise
effects, not causes.

In the effort to account for the causes of Sleep many theories have
been devised. They fall into the two main classes of humoral and
neural hypotheses. All of the first kind rely upon the primary idea of
the production, accumulation and elimination of some substance in
the blood stream whose varying proportions produce the sleep-waking
cycle. Some theorists have selected actual chemical substances for the
role, while others have relied upon purely imaginary materials that
might possess the required characteristics theoretically.

Thus Dubois (21) chose CO_2 as his sleep-producing agent, assuming its increase to cause Sleep and a further increase to bring about
Waking. The obvious difficulty is that no means is provided, or even
suggested, whereby the CO_2 tension, already raised continuously
during these processes, is ever brought back to a level whence the
cycle may be initiated again.

In another theory Pièron (21) (22) selected a hypothetical 'hypnotoxin' circulating in the cerebrospinal fluid but was unable to produce any good evidence for it or to identify it chemically. And to all other such toxic theories there are many objections, some pointed out by Kleitman (*op. cit.*). In the first place the circulation of these substances appears doubtful, if not impossible, as is shown in the cases of two-headed monsters and Siamese twins, one of whom may be sleeping while the other is awake, despite a shared circulation. Furthermore, the curve of sleepiness is not continuous when the subject stays awake for several days, as would be implied; there is greater sleepiness during the night hours and conspicuously less on the afternoon of the third day. Also, if we presume varying concentrations of any toxic substance, there must occur an optimum tension for waking performance, presumably at some time during the day; and if this be so, then during the nightly elimination of the toxic accumulation a similar optimum tension must occur, for which no evidence is found. When we add to this the ascertained datum of poor performance upon waking, when any toxin should be at its lowest concentration, we shall find it difficult to embrace this special kind of Sleep theory.

Other humoral theories emphasize endocrine secretions. Typical of these is that of Salmon, (24), who hypothesized the anterior hypophysis as yielding an antitoxic hormone affecting a diencephalic sleep center. Most of the above objections apply here and in particular it is found that extirpation of the hypophysis causes neither continuous sleep nor waking, thus throwing doubt upon all other theories besides Salmon's which attribute sleep to that gland.

In addition there are sympathetic and parasympathetic theories such as those of Hess (9) (10) and of Stevenson, Christensen and Wortis, (26), which seek the cause of sleep in these functions. Here Kleitman again points out that sympathetic and parasympathetic symptoms are not the cause of sleep, even though they may accompany it, for stimulation of the sympathetic system does not increase wakefulness. These investigators once more are confusing the accompanying symptoms of sleep with its essential nature.

The ideas of Duval and Cajal (13) are typical of many which seek the cause of sleep in the blocking or interruption of neural pathways, some locating such interference at one point, others at different points. Duval and Cajal assumed dendritic retraction on the part of the cells of the cerebral cortex, and a later elongation as a result of strong afferent stimulation. The difficulty is that no investigator has succeeded in demonstrating any movement either of the neurones themselves or of the adjacent neuroglia cells that support them.

Pavlov's view that sleep is a form of widespread cortical inhibition has been criticized by many, among them Kleitman, (13), Nachmansohn (17), Pièron (op. cit.), Liddell, Anderson and James (15). Such critics urge that inhibition is, by definition, the depression of one area by another and that, with such widespread inhibition as is assumed, no area remains as an inhibitory center; that conditioned animal behavior resembles hypnosis rather than sleep; that dogs fall asleep in laboratory situations in the absence of any conditioned stimulus and also while manifesting a conditioned response; that with the whole cortex inhibited there could be no dreaming; and that sleep occurs both in decorticated dogs and in decorticated monkeys. These objections are surely fatal to the Pavlonian theory.

The theory of Claparède (6) (7) views sleep as an 'instinct' and the condition as brought about by a loss of interest in the environment, while waking is brought about by a loss of interest in sleep. Such a speculation hardly deserves serious criticism. It can be said only that 'instinct' is neither a condition nor a thing but an abstraction, that it derives from a different world of discourse than does the term, sleep, and that "interest", either in the environment or in sleep, is too general a word to have any accurate scientific meaning.

Among these neural theories there is a very general one which infers the existence of some specifically localized region whence the whole range of sleep phenomena is initiated or under whose direct control it occurs. The list of such theorists is long and impressive and, although many of these workers introduce modifications and qualifications of their own, they may be classified according to the different regions that they favor, as follows:

SLEEP CENTERS

location

periventricular grey —
  Mauthner

diencephalic region —
  v. Economo
  Pötzl
  Jacarelli & Tsuitsui
  Adler
  Koslowsky
  Pette
  Skliar
  Roger
  Lhermitte
  Sendrail
  Retif
  Marmesco, Sager,
    Kreindler
  Freman
  Ravina
  Devic & Morin
  Schwab
  Gautier

thalamus —
  Trömmer
  Hirsch
  Spiegel
  Friedmann
  Tizzano
  Hechst

cerebral cortex —
  Luksch
  Brailowsky
  Salmon
  Keeser & Keeser
  Fraser-Harris
  Johnson

near oculomotor nuclei —
  Frank
  Stockert
  Kahn

undefined —
  Leyser
  Symonds
  Miles & Laslett
  Palmieri

location

mesodiencephalic region —	undefined —
Jarkowsky	Haenel
Adrian	Ranson
Kleitman	Epstein
	Taussig

These identifications have not passed unchallenged; among those who have declared that they see no reason for assigning a special center for sleep phenomena, since the function is a general organic one, are Adie (1), Byrne (5), Meyer (16), Wechsler (27), Salkind (23), Nachmansohn (17), Altschuler (2) and Spadolini (25). Presumably they would say the same about a waking center, for the controversy between those who assume a sleep center and those who assume a waking one, is minor contrasted with the choice between any center at all or none at all.

The writer confesses that his opinion runs with those of the gentlemen last mentioned. Both Sleep and Waking are general functions at least of the entire organism, certainly to as great an extent as are political activity or general benevolence. Many specific localizations have been discovered for subordinate or part-functions such as hearing, speaking, motor activity and the like, but we would scarcely think of looking for a political center or a general benevolence center. On what grounds, then, should we foresee some special region controlling Sleep and Waking?

It is true that one region has been found, and one only, the supraoptic and paraventricular area of the hypothalamus, where even weak stimulation will abolish consciousness. But Sleep is not identical with the loss of consciousness nor is Waking identical with its presence; they are levels of consciousness, which is quite a different matter. And while this specific region is doubtless in a somewhat different condition when those two different levels occur, it does not follow that its role is either initiatory or controlling. And even if some other symptomatically reacting region be found, the fact that characteristic responses of the region *accompany* Sleep, does not argue that they *cause* it, as has been explained previously in connection with the sympathetic and parasympathetic symptoms of Sleep and Waking. The confusion here again seems to be that between symptoms and causes.

Kleitman, frequently mentioned above, calls his own theory of Sleep 'evolutionary' (14). He views the sleeping condition as primal and distinguishes between wakefulness-of-necessity, brought about by hunger pangs, excretory functions and the like, and wakefulness-of-choice, which is a prolongation of the former condition and becomes established as the cortex increases not only phylogenetically but onto-genetically. The last condition is followed inevitably by Sleep, which is brought about by various kinds of fatigue, thus establishing the sleep-waking rhythm.

There is a long list of objections to this theory also, among them the following: the persistence of sleep-waking rhythms in situations markedly different from those in which they were established, thus showing conditioning not to be a prime cause of rhythm; the occurrence of cataplexy (sudden and complete muscular relaxation accompanied by consciousness) and of catalepsy (hypertonus combined with loss of consciousness), both of which conditions are contrary to prediction in the case of this theory; the fact that deliberate muscular relaxation by itself does not cause Sleep, as should be the case in the premises; the fact that wakefulness-of-necessity involves critical activity at least to some degree, contrary to assertion; and the reversal under certain conditions both of the predicted unpleasantness of wakefulness-of-necessity and of the predicted pleasantness of wakefulness-of-choice. Although this theory has been built from a great many empirical findings, no evidence is available for the confirmation of its logically necessary consequences. It certainly cannot be accepted as a final explanation of the Sleep state for, as Kleitman himself observes, following Pièron: *"Une théorie n'est pas la solution d'un problème; c'est au contraire l'énoncé d'un problème à résoudre."*

Especially in the neural theories mentioned above we find frequent repetition of an idea adopted by numerous investigators of the phenomena of sleep, namely, the idea of the occurrence of blockages within the nervous system during the Sleep state. To the best of the writer's knowledge no direct neurological evidence of such blockages has ever been produced and it has therefore been fashionable to refer to the inferred event as a 'functional' block. It is to be feared that this expression is a circumlocution, like references to so-called 'silent' areas of the cortex, which remain silent only until someone has found out what goes on in them, whereafter the term, silent, is dropped unobtrusively. If anyone demonstrates a genuine nervous system block during Sleep, then 'functional' in this false sense will be dropped also and the term, organic, substituted for it. Such usage of the term, functional, is incorrect, analogical and unjustified; what is meant, is not "functional" but "inferred."

The truth seems to be that the only point at which interruption of the nervous circuits during Sleep can be inferred rigorously with proper justification, is at the thalamic level, or even lower at the level of the medulla, and that this inference applies chiefly to afferent input. There is also some evidence for efferent block in the occurrence of a positive Babinski in deep sleep; this reflex, which in the adult is a diagnostic sign of actual lesion of the pyramidal (motor) tracts, suggests a slight, because easily reversible, block of the efferent pathways from the cortex. Mere frequent scratching of the sole of the foot abolishes it. Further such suggestions lie in the probable decrease during Sleep of reflex reinforcement from higher centers and the usual absence of the righting reflexes, whereas pupillary reflexes are preserved, as well as the lower (autonomic) reflexes governing heart rate, blood pressure, vasomotor and respiratory activity.

In other words, the preserved reflexes are those within one or the other of the two higher divisions of the nervous system, while those absent are interdivisional reflexes or those of the lowest (spinal) division. The spinal cord division of the nervous system shows decrement or absence of the knee jerk and cutaneous reflexes wholly within it and thus is distinguished from the two chief divisions above it. There is therefore a certain amount of evidence of both afferent and efferent blocking during Sleep but these blocks seem to be mainly interdivisional, as if the close connections between the three chief divisions of the nervous system were impeded in some way.

The evidence for afferent block, although inferred rather than directly neurological, is fairly impressive. It will be remembered that in the sensory portion of the nervous system afferent impulses of the second transmittory degree are received at the thalamic synapses; during Sleep they appear never to get beyond this point and it is quite possible that they never reach it, being interrupted at or near the medullar boundary between the spinal cord and head brain divisions. This inference, arising from dream phenomena, is sufficiently interesting to be pursued further.

First it is necessary briefly to analyze the phenomenon of imagery. Stimulation of the receptors results in the transmission of nervous impulses to the thalamus through the spinal cord or, in the cases of the eye, the ear and the nose, through their own specialized transmission tracts, the visual, the auditory and the olfactory. These impulses are then transmitted to the cortex where, to take the case of vision, they have their primary arrival platforms along the calcarene fissure at the back of the head in Brodmann's Area 17 and their final arrival platforms in the adjacent Area 18; further associative connections exist with Area 19 which is a correlation, not a sensory, center.

Thence these already highly integrated visual impulses are projected to still further correlation centers of the cortex.

But at primary arrival platforms, entering afferent impulses yield only raw sensations (of color, tone, pressure, and so on), the crudest form of imagery; and this type of imagery is noticeably absent from dream, which is filled with object-images. The image of an object is a correlation function. Let us take an apple, for example: its image is not an additive combination of redness, roundness, weight and detail of form but of all of these as an object, an integration of the sensory qualities making up something different from, and more than, their sum.

Now during the Waking state nerve impulses of sensory type are coming into the cortex at the rate of some 50 to 100 per second per sensory nerve fiber, and very large numbers of such nerve fibers are operating simultaneously. But during Sleep most of the tremendous sensory input to the cortex is cut off and this breaking of the connections of sensory input with its final arrival platforms is one of the most striking phenomena of Sleep; it is, in fact, the afferent block we have been discussing. It means that sensory stage 8 of our previous analysis is no longer available as the raw material of passive sensory experience.

It is then to be asked how people can experience the rich imagery—visual, auditory, tactile, and so on—of dream during Sleep. The answer is a simple one: our dream images are not the current images of the external world (as we well know) but, instead, they are the remembered images so originated. It is then further asked how these past images are stimulated during Sleep, if they are not aroused as usual through the eye, the ear and other receptors.

This answer is not difficult, either. During Sleep the cortex remains functional and it is in the cortex that the correlation centers are located whose reverberating circuits mediate the memory function. Moreover, innumerable nerve tracts exist through which the nerve impulses of the cortex may stimulate the final arrival platforms of the sensory system, which thus are able to operate, during Sleep, from internal cortical stimuli rather than from externally originated receptor stimuli, as during Waking.

If this be the case, we find an immediate solution for the well-recognized 'irrational' content of our dream sequences. For 'rational' content means only that the sequences of Waking sensory experience are controlled strictly by the sequences of external sensory input, which in turn must follow and be determined by the sequences of the objective phenomena of outside environment. When the latter are interrupted by the afferent block occurring during Sleep, the dream experience is released from this external control and it then follows the logics of emotion and intellection but no longer the practical logic of external event. The ordinary man confuses rationality with practical logic but the latter is not the only sort of logic existing, as is evident from at least the partial success of logical dream interpretation as practiced by psychoanalysts and others.

However, we are still left with the problem of the afferent block itself during Sleep, and probably with that of an efferent block, too. The afferent block seems a necessary inference from the absence of current sensory stimulation from the phenomena of dream (except in special and unusual instances) and already we have noticed the evidence for efferent block. Both inferences imply a partial severance of the spinal cord system from the head brain and basal gangliar systems during Sleep and the organic field measurements in Sleep also differentiate between the former and the two latter systems.

The spinal cord field division yields a U-curve of activity during Sleep, which corresponds with many other activity-curves of sleep-function and is to be expected, since most of these other U-curve activities are closely connected with spinal cord phenomena. But with the head brain field division we find a gradually falling curve during the entire course of Sleep and with the autonomic field division no particular tendency in either direction, as if the latter represented a compromise between the other two activities. In any case the fall in activity to the midpoint of the sleeping period and then its gradual recovery, still during Sleep, until approximately the original level is reached at the end of the period, is absent from the two higher divisions of the nervous system.

But none of this is seen in the measurements of the Waking control subjects and it is thus evident that the spinal cord field division follows a quite different course from the others during Sleep. That this difference is closely connected with the blocking phenomenon discussed, has not been ascertained but the difference suggests the possibility that these blocks may be related to the respective field forces affecting the three systems differently during the Sleep state.

Actually there is strong probability that the field forces involved are responsible for the interdivisional block during Sleep, although this cannot be said to have been demonstrated fully. But of the various Sleep theories which we have noted, none of them has accounted fully, or even satisfactorily, for the instatement of the Sleep state or the ensuing reinstatement of the Waking state.

The Sleep state can be described partially by listing its symptoms but it cannot be defined by them. Nor can it be defined by theories alleging its cause or causes; causes are one thing and what they cause, is something else entirely. For this reason humoral, neural and similar hypotheses as to the cause of Sleep do not define its nature, although they may (if partially correct) suggest to us certain necessary characteristics of that nature.

But the chief objection to the various causal theories so far noticed is that all of them select certain minor part-reactions of the organism and seek through them to account for a resultant condition applying to the organism as a whole. Sleep is a general, not a local, condition and pervades not simply the entire organism but the whole economy of the entire human being as such, including the subjective factor which is the 'I'-entity and its state of consciousness. But since at present we must deal with this factor, the 'I'-entity, only in its postulated condition as I_c, it will be better to return to the objective organism and to account for the Sleep state from that direction.

It has been suggested by others that Sleep reflects the magnetic disconnection of the three brain systems and, if so, this disruption of a magnetic tie between the systems would account not only for the interdivisional block during Sleep but for the state itself. Moreover, it would constitute not a cause of Sleep but, instead, it would *define* the condition known to us as Sleep. We submit that this magnetic disruption *is* the real physiological definition of the Sleep state.

The organic field of the body is an electro-*magnetic* field, as are the subfields of the three chief brain systems. The alteration both of the general organic field and of its component subfields has been demonstrated in the Sleep state and it has been shown that the subfields follow different and independent (i.e., disconnected) patterns during Sleep. We may have here an explanation both of so-called functional block during Sleep and of the internally rather than externally stimulated dream phenomena, as we would expect if the head brain were disconnected magnetically, especially from the spinal brain. In our own situation, however, the magnetic disruption is not total; the basal gangliar-cerebral magnetic bond is not broken to any great degree and thus internally stimulated cerebral dream expresses and releases basal gangliar affective (emotional) energies. This only partial disconnection, resulting from the unbalanced expenditure of our Waking energies, in turn defines our abnormal Sleep.

And indeed Sleep is closely related to our organic energies. It is generally agreed that sleeping is a recuperative process. What is recuperated? The organism comprises the three factors of its chemical constituents, its thermodynamic energies and its biological organic DC field. In the present case it is the second or positive factor, the organic energies, with which we have to deal. These are exactly what are recuperated and replenished during Sleep.

This is not to say that digestion cannot take place also during the Waking state. Indeed, as we shall see in coming chapters, the more important of our assimilative processes can occur only when the subjective entity is more fully awake than usual, for these processes can be brought about solely by an unusual activity on the part of the 'I'-entity itself during the efforts to alter the Waking state to one of Awakeness.

But in the ordinary Waking state the digestive activity is entirely that of the organism and this activity during Waking is only partially as effective as it is during Sleep. All sorts of external Waking stimuli interfere with it, whereas in Sleep the reception of these stimuli is greatly diminished and there is much less interruption of the anabolic processes *per se*.

As the Integrative psychologist would put it, the organism's Hunger Drive comprises the successive responses of Desire and Satisfaction toward food. Desire is a compound response of active Dominance-passive Compliance toward the food during its ingestion, which later, during digestion, alters to one of passive Dominance-active Compliance, as the food itself begins to master the organism's responses. (18).

This effect is to be seen plainly after a large meal, when the reciprocal effects of the food upon the organism during digestion are manifested. Blood then tends to be directed toward the alimentary canal and away from the brain and the skeletal musculature; lethargy and drowsiness set in and the passively registrant 'I'-entity may succumb automatically and indulge in a nap.

This is a more interesting phenomenon than may appear ordinarily. In the first place it shows the organism tending toward the Sleep state as the optimum condition for digestion. In the second place it testifies to the efficacy of the technique of non-identified observation previously described (and is sometimes employed as an objective measure of it), for the solely observational activity of the 'I'-entity under these conditions can—and when exercised effectively, does—

abolish the tendency toward Sleep, while at the same time assisting and speeding up the assimilative process sensorily observed.

However, we are speaking now only of passively conscious man. In his case and in the absence of activity by the subjective entity it is evident that Sleep is the optimum condition for digestion and, through it, for the replenishment of the organism's energies.

There are two different ways of viewing the energy sources required for our full range of activities, including the mental, the emotional and the practical or 'physical'. The first and customary way is to account for all of our energies from the first three steps of the digestive process only, the transformation of our ordinary food through the three stages of the solid, the liquid and the gaseous. This accounts for our ordinary 'physical' energies and it is then assumed that mental and emotional phenomena take place simply as the by-products of the functioning organic system, especially of its neural operations.

The inadequacies of such a view are plain. It is entirely silent regarding the sources of our mental and emotional energies and it renders no account even of the neural energies involved, which are certainly quite different from muscular energies, for instance.

It is fashionable to say that the human body is a mechanism for the transformation of electrical energy. Taking this proposition seriously, let us ask whence these electrical energies come. No actual little dynamos have ever been found within the human organism but that electrical energies are present within it, cannot be doubted. All neural activity not only depends upon but actually comprises electrical energy and both the AC and the DC phenomena of the body have long been recognized and measured.

The solid-liquid-gaseous view also leaves us with the shaky proposition that a full gastrointestinal tract must provide us *ipso facto* with the mental energies required for advanced mathematics and the emotional energies for symphonic procreation. There are many contradictions in this idea, among them the fact that very hungry people have contributed to mathematical discovery and to musical composition. It is clear that a new approach to the question is demanded, for both substances and energies beyond the solid, the liquid and the gaseous states of matter clearly are required for the exercise of functions more subtle than the purely muscular.

What, then, are the energy sources of the human organism? It does not manufacture its various energies out of nothing and there is no mystery as to the origin of the relevant raw materials. It is from nourishment that the organic energies of the human body are derived by means of its intake and the subsequent metabolic processes to which it is subjected by and within the organism. Nourishment consists of the various sorts of food ingested by the body.

But the nourishments absorbed by the human body may not be quite so simple and restricted as the dietician usually assumes; and it is possible that they pass through more digestive stages than those with which gross physiology deals. It is necessary first to examine all the actual stages of organic metabolism before we can describe properly the replenishment period of organic recuperation which is Sleep.

The complete list of chemical substances derived by the body from the nourishments it takes in, would be extremely long, comprising not only the simpler elements like iron, salts and so on, but many compound and complex substances necessary for glandular and neural operation. Not all of them are known accurately to modern physiology. But in any case these chemical constituents of the body comprise only the negative factor in its total economy and it is the positive factor, the energies, of which we must treat here.

In the outline to follow, therefore, we shall be concerned primarily with energies and with the general physical stages or steps of the anabolic (building up) process, it being taken for granted that within each step various specific chemical products may be elaborated contemporaneously. Anabolism makes up one-half of metabolism; it is the constructive half, whereas katabolism, the other half, is concerned with the assemblage and disposal of the body's waste products. The energies present in our foods are extracted from the latter by the organism during the anabolic process.

This process begins with the intake through the mouth of the solid and liquid materials which, when necessary, are masticated, mixed with saliva and swallowed, thus passing through the esophagus and into the stomach. There they are subjected to a series of reactions with the chemicals present in that organ—reactions that have already begun with the saliva in the mouth—and the results pass through the sphincter at the base of the stomach and thus enter the small intestine through the pyloris.

Here the digestive processes begun in mouth and stomach are continued by the bile and pancreatic juices, and the still altering substances pass through the cecum to the large intestine. The walls of both intestines are composed of mucous membranes in which are embedded capillaries, veins and lacteal glands of the circulatory system, through which the products of digestion are absorbed directly into the blood stream. At this point the raw material originally taken in is represented in three different conditions or states, solid, liquid and gaseous, all of which are characteristic not only of the substances themselves but contain also the comparable organic energies such, for example, as heat.

Anabolism, like many other basic processes, follows the course of an octave; its stages comprise seven steps, like the musical scale from 'do' through re, mi, fa, sol, la and si to the next originating 'do'. During such octavic progressions, between the third and fourth stages (mi and fa) and the seventh and eighth stages (si and the next 'do'), external reinforcements or 'shocks' are required for the further progression of the transformations. Up to the present point in the anabolic process the first three steps—solid, liquid and gaseous—have been completed and the substances and their energies are now in the venous blood at the stage, mi, where external reinforcement is demanded.

The portal vein brings this blood, together with its contents, into the liver.

There it encounters the pulmonary blood arriving from the lungs and carrying with it the absorbed gases from the pulmonary circulation through the lungs and heart. This blood, rich in oxygen and other absorbed gases, furnishes the required reinforcement for the further anabolism of the partially digested content entering the liver through the portal vein from the gastrointestinal tract, at least some of it now also in the gaseous state.

These latter substances with their energies, consisting of the first form of organic food, will now complete their sevenfold anabolism and, in doing so, must pass through four further states. The substances elaborated within the limits of these latter states of matter will yield the types of organic energies respectively required for motational, mental, emotional and procreative activities.

Thus it is seen that the substances we take in as our first form of food, must pass through anabolic and digestive stages beyond the gaseous and it is from such substances in their further progressive transformations that we derive the energies demanded for functions beyond the merely muscular. This first octave of digestive steps furnishes the full range of energy supplies demanded for our ordinary activities and these energies are then increased by the first three steps of the digestion of the substances in the inhaled air that we breathe and which then will pass through their own first three digestive stages automatically. But at that point the air octave must cease its own progression in the absence of reinforcement from outside its own range.

At this juncture a third form of food is available to us but abnormal men do not utilize it. Thus no effect is produced such as might otherwise furnish a shock for the air octave, and the latter dies out after its third stage of digestion has been reached. Nevertheless, all the energies demanded for the automatic behavior of mechanical men already have been provided and no more are required in order to explain the contrasted states of Sleep and Waking in which such men exist.

Since the Sleep state is concerned with the recuperation of the presently utilized energies of the organism, we now have a more rational account than hitherto of its natural function and of its general nature. The first form of food, the oral, is taken in intermittently; the second form, the nasal, is taken in continually; and the third form, not being taken in at all, can be disregarded for the moment.

The period of Sleep of course is not concerned primarily with acquiring the food supplies but rather with elaborating from them the requisite organic energies. If we suppose Sleep to serve such a designed purpose in accordance with the human paradic, its suitability to this end is apparent immediately. It is a period of quiescence so far as concerns the striped musculature, the mechanical agency for dealing with the changing external environment; and in general the organism, having arranged temporarily for a non-menacing environment during Sleep (or in any case being forced to assume such conditions), is mostly shut off from outside stimulation. The anabolic processes are chiefly spinal cord functions and so not only is the afferent nervous system block during Sleep adapted to the release of the higher centers from constant external stimuli but the block on the efferent side of the arc will afford to the spinal cord mechanisms a relative freedom from interference from above, so that they can fulfill their primary function during Sleep of recuperating the organic energies later necessary for Waking performance.

Many of the ascertained characteristics of Sleep have just these desired effects. Among them we may notice closure of the eyelids, relaxation of the skeletal musculature, diminution of action potentials, decrease in reinforcement from higher centers, instatement of the positive Babinski in deep sleep (evidencing efferent block), absence of effect upon digestive processes or upon gastric and intestinal motility or the secretion of bile, decrease in basal heat production, increase in blood volume, decrease in heart rate and blood pressure, presence of thoracic rather than abdominal breathing, and the afferent block already mentioned. Both the AC brain wave measurements and the DC field measurements with their relatively steady, unwavering graph lines likewise evidence a resting, recuperative condition of the organism and a minimum of interaction among the three chief divisions of the nervous system.

The chief interference with this beneficial period of restfulness and recuperative function arises from the phenomena of dream, and we have already traced this occurrence to the abnormality of the preceding Waking state in which the energies of the organism are expended in an unbalanced and disharmonious fashion. This habitual misuse of our ordinary energies has reached such a degree of maladjustment that a recent investigation at Mount Sinai Hospital in New York (8) suggests that dream deprivation leads to serious anxiety and agitation, loss of bodily weight and, if carried far enough, to a serious disruption of the entire personality. Far from asserting the benefit of dreaming, however, these findings are a measure of the abnormality of the previous Waking state from which the necessity for dreaming arises; and they reinforce the opinion that our passively registrant state of consciousness is a distorted and unnatural one.

From the point of view of our own position all of these considerations go to show that the organic conditions characteristic of Sleep indicate a resting, energy-recuperating period implicit in the human paradic but that these conditions are met only approximately, never fully, in our present situation. As to the whole economy of the human being, the 'I'-entity at its state of I_0, only passively conscious during the preceding period of Waking, as a result obtains little rest during Sleep but, instead, continuing its passive registration of the now properly non-integrated end-products of neural functioning, assists in disrupting and in interfering with the normal process of actual organic recuperation.

We may then describe the paradic Sleep state as one of quiescence and relative unrelatedness to the external environment, during which anabolic processes restore the organic energies previously depleted and in which the 'I'-entity, one of the basic factors in the whole human economy, lapses into a state of unconsciousness.

The abnormal counterpart of Sleep—which we experience—may be described as a deformed substitute for this paradic state, in which dream stimuli take the place of external environment in initiating organic responses, in which consequently the proper anabolic processes of a paradic nature are interrupted and full organic recuperation prevented, and in which the factor representing the 'I'-entity continues intermittently its passive responses to the end-products of neural function furnished by the dream phenomena of the organism.

As this pseudo-Sleep is related closely to the preceding Waking state (which itself constitutes a pseudo-Awakeness), we may now proceed to a description of the latter.

REFERENCES IN THE TEXT OF CHAPTER IV

1) Adie, W. J.　　Idiopathic narcolepsy: a disease sui generis, with remarks on the mechanism of sleep. *Brain*, 1926, 49: 257-306.

2) Altschuler, I. M.　　Sleep and epidemic encephalitis. *J Neurol. & Psychopath.*, 1917, 9: 222-227.

3) Burr, H. S.　　Field properties of the developing frog's egg. *Proc. Nat'l. Acad. of Sciences*, 1941, 27: 276-281.

4) Burr, H. S. and Northrop, F.S.C.　　Evidence for the existence of an electrodynamic field in living organisms. *Proc. Nat'l. Acad. of Sciences*, 1939, 25: 284-288.

5) Byrne, J. G.　　*Studies of the physiology of the eye: still reaction, sleep, dreams, hibernation, repression, hypnosis, narcosis, coma and allied conditions.* H. K. Lewis & Co., Ltd., London, 1933: p. 428.

6) Claparède, E.   La Question de sommeil. *Année psychol.*, 1912: 419-459.

7) Claparède, E.   La sommeil et la veille. *J. de psychol.*, 1928, 26: 113-174.

8) Dement, W.   The effect of sleep deprivation. *Science*, 10 June, 1960, 131: 1705-1707.

9) Hess, W. R.   The mechanism of sleep. *Am. J. Physiol.*, 1929, 90: 386-387.

10) Hess, W. R.   Der Schlaf. *Klin. Wchnschr.*, 1933, 12: 129-134.

11) King, C. D.   Electrometric studies of sleep. *J. Gen. Psychol.*, 1946, 35: 131-159.

12) Kleitman, N.   *Sleep and Wakefulness.* Univ. Chic. Press, 1939, Chapters II-VIII.

13) Kleitman, N.   Ibid., pp. 469-471.

14) Kleitman, N.   Ibid., pp. 502 ff.

15) Liddell, H. S.,   An examination of Pavlov's theory of internal inhibition.
    Anderson, O. D.   *Am. J. Physiol.*, 1929, 90: 430-431.
    and James, W. T.

16) Meyer, E.   Uber organische Nervenkrankungen in Gefolge von Grippe. *Arch, f. Psychiat.*, 1921, 62: 598-626.

17) Nachmansohn, D.   Zur Frage des Schlafzentrums: Eine Betrachtung der Theorien über Entstehung des Schlafes. *Ztschr. f. d. ges. Neurol. u. Psychiat.*, 1927, 107: 342-401.

18) Marston, W. M.   *Integrative Psychology,* Kegan Paul, Trench, Trubner,
    King, C. D., and   London, 1931: pp. 172-178.
    Marston, E. H.

19) Pavlov, I. P.   The identity of inhibition with sleep and hypnosis. *Sci. Monthly*, 1923, 17: 603-608.

20) Pavlov, I. P.   *Conditioned reflexes: an investigation of the physiological activity of the cerebral cortex.* Oxford Univ. Press. N.Y., 1927: p. 430.

21) Pièron, H.   *Le problème physiologique du sommeil.* Masson & Cie., Paris, 1913: p. 520.

22) Pièron, H.   Discussion du rapport de Jean Lhermitte et Auguste Tournay: le sommeil normal et pathologique. *Rev. Neurol.* 1927, (I): 830-832.

23) Salkind, E.   Zur Pathogenese des Schlafes nach Beobachtungen bei der epidemischen Encephaliyis. *Sovet. psikhonevrol.*, 1925, 1: 32-44.

24) Salmon, A.   Il centro diencefalico regolatore del sonno. *Scritti. med. in onore Gabbi*, 1930, (I): 132-146.

25) Spadolini, N.   Alcune considerzioni sulla fisiologia e fisiopatologia del sonno. *Note e riv. di psichiat.*, 1930, 55: 283-290.

26) Stevenson, L.,   Some experiments in intercranial pressure during sleep
    Christensen, B. E. and under certain other conditions. *Am. J. M. Sc.*, 1929,
    and Wortis, S. B.   178: 663-677.

27) Wechsler   Discussion of tumors of the third ventricle. *Arch. Neurol. & Psychiat.*, 1928, 20: 1404.

chapter V

WAKING

VERY LITTLE WORK HAS BEEN DONE on the physiological conditions of the Waking state as such, although of course there is a great amount of data on various subdivisions of the body during this period.

Specific AC brain wave rhythms have been identified as characteristic of the Waking state and individuals have been typed as alphas or betas in that condition. In this connection it is interesting to note that brain wave forms accompanying the hypnotic state correspond to the Waking rhythms rather than to those of Sleep. And the DC tracings of the relatively rapid fluctuations of the organic field in all three major subdivisions of the nervous system permit us in this respect to make a sharp distinction between the Waking and Sleep states.

But in general it seems simply to be taken for granted that Waking is the normal (in the false sense of usual or average) state for human beings and in fact the Dictionary of Psychology (1) defines "wake" as "to remain in the normal condition of consciousness, as contrasted with sleep." In Gould's Medical Dictionary (4) the word is not even mentioned.

Little could be more unsatisfactory than this cavalier treatment of the matter and the Dictionary of Psychology is sadly in error when it implies the normality of the Waking state. Disregarding the subsidiary neurotic and psychotic conditions investigated by psychology, themselves variations of the Waking state, there is no general level of consciousness for human beings so abnormal objectively as Waking. It may even be surmised that certain other states of consciousness, miscalled abnormal merely because they are unusual, are less abnormal objectively than is the Waking state.

One symptom of the abnormality of the Waking state is evidenced just above: it is the irrational suggestibility whereby we all convince each other that the Waking condition is a healthy and proper one, for no other reason than that we are all its common victims. These statements become fully clear, once we have redefined the normal or paradic as that which functions in accordance with its inherent design.

In approaching a physiological description of the Waking state we must return for a moment to the question of the energies utilized by the human organism, those energies which are replenished during the state of Sleep. A more detailed account of the nature of this complete range of energies than was given in the preceding chapter, is called for now.

It will be remembered that the first three stages of the digestion of our first (oral) food have been completed when these partially anabolized substances enter the blood stream from the intestines and are carried to the liver through the portal vein. Some of these substances and their energies are used for the current operations of the body, while another portion, now encountering the gaseous substances in the pulmonary circulation, receives the shock or reinforcement necessary for its further anabolic transformations. It is of these further transformations that we must now speak.

The substances resulting from such anabolic transformations beyond the gaseous state are not investigated seriously today and so they remain relatively unknown to us, despite our probable possession of the techniques and instrumentation required for their accurate identification. But we are not unacquainted with some of the states of matter in which these substances exist. The best known of them are the magnetic and electrical states.

The work of Burr and his associates (2) over some forty years has demonstrated conclusively that living systems are characterized by steady-state electrical fields which both determine and are affected subsequently by the organized properties of their constituent elements. Protoplasm itself exhibits electromagnetic properties. Living cells possess what in a magnet are called north and south poles; and cell boundaries set up potential gradients which both determine and are determined by their own pattern of organization and that of the organism of which they are subordinate parts. The electrical AC properties of such organs as the brain and the heart are measurable accurately by the electroencephalograph and the electrocardiograph; and even ordinary muscle contraction is accompanied by the propagation of an electrical wave. The conduction of the nerve impulse by and through the neurones of the nervous system is basically electrical in character. All these phenomena and a great many others demonstrate that the human organism, not only as a whole but in respect of its parts, possesses magnetic and electrical properties and energies.

It can be said that magnetic and electrical properties are mediated by substances in magnetic and electrical states or alternatively it can be said that magnetism and electricity are themselves substances or forms of matter in their own right. Whichever of these statements we may prefer, it follows that, since these two kinds of energies are demanded for the operation of the human organism, they must be supplied and replenished from the food intake of the organism. Such supplies are furnished by the further anabolic processes of food digestion beyond the gaseous stage at which they enter the liver, either by the transformation of the gaseous substances into magnetic and electrical states (the former view) or by the production from them of further substances called magnetism and electricity (the latter view). In either case the further progression of the digestive process beyond the gaseous stage furnishes the organic substances from which the body obtains its magnetic and electrical properties.

To the reader this may be a novel view and it should be supported further. In the first place all of the food intake of the body, both oral and nasal, contains electricity, of which magnetism is a component. No physicist would deny that oatmeal, beefsteak or oxygen contains protons, electrons, neutrons, and so on.

The process of digestion consists in the *extraction* by the body of the various entities contained in the ingested food. The first three steps of anabolism (of the oral food) extract chemical entities in solid, liquid and gaseous form, leaving the food products still with their magnetic and electrical components intact.

Those steps beyond the first three, in turn extract magnetism and electricity from the selfsame ingested food products. As regards the nasal food intake, already in the gaseous state when it reaches the liver, its immediately following digestive stages extract from it the same magnetism and electricity that is procured from the oral food after *its* gaseous stage has been utilized. As to the oral food, two further substances or energies are extracted from it, the cardiac and genetic, but the nasal food extraction remains unreinforced and thus stalled after the electrical stage is reached.

These operations of anabolism account in a rational way for the presence of magnetism, electricity and further products of digestion in the functioning organism, which surely is better than leaving the full energy resources of the body unaccounted for, even theoretically. For we cannot doubt that the body does possess magnetic, electrical and procreative energies, that it does not contain any miniature dynamos for the transformation of these energies directly from the surrounding atmosphere and therefore that such energies must be anabolized from the intake of the substances generally called food. There is no other source for them.

As to the distinction between energies and substances during the anabolic processes, this distinction, though correct, is chiefly a matter of convenience, for of course both energies and substances are produced. Regarding the last stage, the genetic, of the oral digestion no one doubts that procreative *energies* are extracted; they account for ordinary bisexual behavior and, on a higher level, for the correct or incorrect love responses between the two sexes. Similarly there is no question that procreative *substances* are produced at this stage—the male sperm and the female ovum. Since magnetism and electricity are at the same time states of matter, i.e., substances, and also mediate the comparable energies, the situation is the same in their cases as in that of genetic substances and energies.

It was a proposition of the Institute earlier mentioned that the magnetic stage was produced at the solar plexus level and the electrical stage at that of the cerebrum. As this proposition has never been verified, or even investigated scientifically, for the moment it must remain hypothetical. The same is equally true of the proposition that, beyond the electrical stage, two further anabolic transformations take place at the loci of the heart complex and of the sex glands, furnishing respectively those substances and energies required for highly evolved emotional responses and for the production of chromosomal and genetic entities with their tremendously complex hereditary characteristics and their equally tremendous reproductive capabilities. The Institute, of course, stated these propositions not as hypotheses but as facts, while insisting that for the student in his present condition they must remain hypothetical.

But whatever our attitude toward these statements of detailed localization, one aspect of them is certain: that magnetic, electrical and genetic energies are produced in the human organism and that these must come from the anabolic processes to which its food intake is subjected following ingestion. That these processes follow an octavic pattern and thus, all told, produce the full seven stages of digestive progression, can scarcely be doubted, since (with the possible exception of the cardiac stage) all seven types of energies are known to be required for the organism's operation.

But if we should account in this way for the full range of energy supplies demanded by the organism and elaborated by it mainly during Sleep for use chiefly during Waking, the properly integrated use of these supplies still must be determined either by the paradic or by the abnormal characteristics of the Waking state itself. And the actual nature of those characteristics must relate directly to the inherent design of the human organism.

An organic mechanism plainly designed for harmonious integration but which is functioning disharmoniously, is manifestly in an abnormal condition; and within the human organism during the Waking state very few elements can be found that are operating harmoniously in accordance with the inherent design of that organism. This is especially true in respect of the neural systems involved, which themselves constitute the integrating mechanism of the body and where the prevailing disharmony is to be seen most plainly. When we realize that the end-products of these very systems furnish the sources of the entire human experience, it will be understood that the ensuing abnormality is not only organic but experiential as well.

During Waking the three chief divisions of the nervous system — the cerebral system, the basal gangliar and autonomic system, and the spinal cord system — are not in harmonious balance with each other but, to the contrary, are in constant opposition and conflict. In any given subject one of these systems usually dominates and controls the other two, in direct contradiction to their organic design. The results are observable both in experience and in behavior, for it is this interior disharmony that produces the three basic and abnormal types of intellectual man, of emotional man and of practical man.

All these types are abnormal, because one becomes an intellectualist only at the expense of his own emotional and practical abilities, an emotionalist only at the expense of intellection and practicality, and a practical person only at the expense both of his intellect and of his emotions. That does not mean that any of these functions is absent but it does mean that, when intellect dominates emotion and practicality, then both of the latter are either stunted or distorted and that the same is true for any other dominance of one system over the others. The artist and the religionist are notoriously infantile in their manipulation of abstract concepts, as is the practical man of affairs, while the genuine intellectualist is equally inept in his handling of practical matters.

These internal disharmonies are reflected accurately in the external animosities plaguing all three types. Indeed they cannot even understand one another properly, let alone succeed in that intersupporting cooperation which is the fundamental background of all really civilized intercourse. All this is very plain indeed when we consider the exaggerated instances of these three basic types; but the unfortunate truth is that every one of us is an example of one such type predominantly and most of the time and that we delude only ourselves when we deny our personal attitudes and prejudices of these kinds. A truly harmonious man in whom all three of his primary functions are balanced in accordance with his own paradic, is never encountered.

When a circumstance as obvious as this one is pointed out, it is typical of persons in the Waking state not only to seek to avoid its acknowledgement but even to attempt rationalizations whereby its plain terms may be denied. Quite recently we have had a solemn instance of this kind of inversion in a serious discussion of the means whereby persons already more lopsided than most others may be encouraged and assisted to indulge and increase their distortions. (6).

Imbalance of this kind also is related closely to the unequal utilization of organic energies in the Waking state. Haphazard external stimuli cause haphazard energy discharges. And added to this is the channelling of the chance discharges through the abnormally predominant system, whichever it may be. It is easy to see, therefore, how the organism comes to the Sleep period with some of its energies exhausted but others expended hardly at all. The latter are quite literally the stuff of which dreams are made.

We have alluded previously to the abnormally reversed behavior sequences that are a feature of the Waking state. In that condition there first occurs some external stimulus or combination of stimuli to which the organism reacts automatically with a response that may be partially suitable but is seldom fully so. This overt response is followed immediately by an emotional response concentrated almost entirely upon the improper elements of the so-called physical reaction. And there then follows the mental reaction of rationalization, seeking to put the blame for the whole occurrence upon someone or something other than the subject.

Let us take an example: a person touches the hot plate of an electric stove. There is an instant retraction of the part of the organism in contact with the plate, a purely reflex reaction. On its heels comes the disagreeable emotional response associated inevitably with the pain sensations produced by the contact. Then comes the mental response: what dolt turned this stove on! Instead of the rational question, why was I wandering around in a semiconscious daydream and putting my hand on this hot plate, there is the immediate attempt to blame someone else for the subject's own subhuman behavior.

It is a simplified example but the reader will be able to recall many more complex ones following the same general sequence of response. The law courts, for instance, are cluttered with cases involving people who have been struck by automobiles while crossing the street in a daze; and how often is the semiconscious victim willing to take even the smallest portion of the blame upon himself? One only can sympathize with the semiconscious judge who finds it his duty to disentangle the respective faults of the semiconscious jaywalker and the semiconscious driver.

The important thing about this behavior sequence, however, is not the abnormality of its separate parts so much as the abnormality of the succession itself. It must be clear that in it the subject is deprived of any decision whatever. The whole occurrence is based first upon external chance or accident and second upon the predetermined series of responses called forth by the nature of the given organism. Apart from delusions of rationalization the subject himself has no say in the matter at all. It is not sometimes but all the time, and most of all when he doesn't know it, that he is the 'victim of circumstances' and of his own uncontrollable machine.

Certainly this is not the portrait of a genuine human being. It denies his human design, it denies his paradic; and we ourselves, who live under just these conditions, cannot fail to be revolted by them as soon as they are stated clearly. If we should ever become fully conscious of them in our own personal experiences, we would be more than revolted, we would be completely dismayed.

Underlying the reversed sequence of behavior in the Waking state there is a reversal of experiential function such that the subject:

1. ignorantly accepts all sorts of misinformation, his views on almost any matter being a hodge-podge of false propositions, i.e., he lacks a critical faculty;

2. is always prejudiced and biased, usually in the most crassly personal ways, i.e., he lacks impartiality;

3. is usually prepared to (and always does) act upon his prejudiced misinformation, i.e., he lacks individual decision.

The last point alone demonstrates that our so-called free will is delusional. As the novelist tells us: "Madness consists in not recognizing facts, in making wishes the fathers of thoughts, in conceiving things to be other than they really are. . . . There is nothing except a swarm of constellated impulses and sentiments and notions; a swarm brought together by the accidents of heredity and language; a swarm of often contradictory thoughts and desires. . . . To talk of freedom in connection with acts which in reality are determined, is madness." (5).

And the biologist adds: "Volition implies some sort of control of its units by the organism, the power to compel ion movements in nerve cells and the discharge of nerve impulses to appropriate muscles. . . . Perhaps our subjective conviction of willing our acts is a complete illusion; certainly it is an almost complete one or else great fields of physiological and psychological evidence are woefully in error." (3).

But these delusions are only symptoms. We have seen that in the Waking state the conscious factor in the human being, the relationship between neural event and subjective experience which is designed as an active one, is in fact almost wholly passive. There is nothing that a man may claim validly to do except to think, to feel or to act. But it is an error to suppose that he really *does* any of this, since all of these activities are based upon neurological events over which he has no control, of which indeed he is unaware.

In the case of sensing it is not the man who activates his own sensory equipment but rather the external environment that originates such activation, after which the results, now translated by organically determined processes and their passive registration in consciousness, then are experienced in subjective terms. In the case of action the result is even more automatic.

That the case is different with the other two categories of experiential content, emotion and thought, is only another delusion, less subtle in the instance of vivid emotion, more subtle in that of the complexities of thought.

Emotion is generated by the basal gangliar and associated operations of the nervous system; and here, too, far from having any control of the operation, the man in question is altogether unaware that it takes place.

Similarly, thought is produced by the cerebral operation of the correlation tracts within the cortex. Then, when the subject registers passively in his experience the mental content that he cannot possibly avoid registering, that subject becomes the victim of the delusion that it is he and not the integrative mechanism of the cerebral centers which has manufactured the experience. His false belief is correct only in that the neurological phenomena could never constitute experience except for his passive registration of them; it is incorrect when the deduction is drawn that they have been more than passively registered, namely, that the registrar himself has also devised the neural integrations.

In the case of so-called original thought, especially of a philosophic or scientific kind, the activity of the integrating centers is great. And it is the *passive* experience of this *active* aspect of the mechanical events which carries over into subjective experience and deludes the subject into supposing the activity to be his own.

Another cause of the false belief in control is the fact that very frequently one subdivision of the integrating mechanism does control the others automatically; and this kind of control, instead of being identified objectively as to its source, is projected by the passive experiencer upon himself. This also is an origin of the three abnormal types of intellectual, emotional and practical man.

But men as we find them in the Waking state, are unaware even of their own gross physical behavior — of the ways in which their bodies move, of the characteristics, for instance, of their physical gaits, of the expressions that others may read flitting across their faces, of the manners in which their voices sound to others, of all the innumerable little physical habits and traits which make up their own real personalities in these respects. They cannot recognize their own bodies in a motion picture or their own voices on a sound track.

People have subjective images of themselves that are illusory. They miss the objective reality entirely and are unable to give an honest description of themselves that would be recognizable by their friends and acquaintances. This sort of existence, literally and strictly, is a kind of sleep-walking, sleep-talking, and so forth, and it demonstrates a passive and meager Waking level of existence, which we cannot fail to admit as objectively abnormal.

Many persons can be brought to an admission of the foregoing truth, and then they make the assumption that what is true in the case of their grossest behavior, is quite otherwise in respect of their emotions and thoughts. They assume that introspection, the very core of subjectivity, provides them with correct information about the quite different basis of their subjective experience, namely, neural phenomena. But just as we should dismiss the claims of a mathematician who asserted his proficiency regarding logarithms while remaining plainly deficient in arithmetic, so we must reject those of a man who, acknowledging his inability to be aware of his most obvious physical behavior, assures us that he is fully cognizant of—nay, even controls—his own emotions and thoughts. To the contrary, we see plainly that he is their victim and for the most part unaware of their occurrence.

He experiences as emotions and thoughts only a small fraction of the basal gangliar and cortical integrations actually present. He does not experience the neurological reality of their occurrence but only the verbalisms reflected from them, and of these he is under the delusion of authorship. This must be so, once we have established that he is unaware of the grosser forms of his bodily behavior, for the ability to be conscious of emotions and thoughts fully and actively (directly and *not* through introspection) is only a higher degree of the ability to be conscious of simpler personal phenomena. If the latter be lacking, so must the former be; and if it be lacking, the situation must be considered as abnormal for any genuine human being.

There are many, many data of experimental psychology which mirror this circumstance. For example, sensory adaptation: we know that the neural mechanisms involved do not fatigue, and it is probable that the sensation disappears because of the sluggish passivity of the subject and his inability to maintain, even for a short time, his meager sensory consciousness.

The so-called smoothing in experiential content of the discrete nerve impulses is another case in point. For if the human subject be the victim of a severe lethargy within his own registration process and posterior to conductive or synaptic phenomena, we should expect just such a smoothing whereby the more minute distinctions of stimulation and conduction were wholly or mostly lost.

Another instance, among many, is the superior visual discrimination of the monkey when compared with man. There is no evidence that its visual apparatus is superior, in fact the opposite is to be shown.

Nor is all that occurs, registered, even passively. From this partial absence of registration arises a whole train of theories about the unconscious, the subconscious, the foreconscious, censors, ids, suppressions, complexes, and so on. All such theories and terms actually refer only to the varying degrees whereby the passively supine subject fails to register, even passively, very many of the neurological integrations constantly going forward under their own steam in the associated nervous system.

It must be recognized that all these terms, such as subconscious and the rest of them, indicate a non-objective, analogical way of thinking and that to all propositions employing them the words, "as if," ought to be prefaced. There is no such real condition as subconsciousness—there is either some real degree of consciousness or there is its real absence—for subconsciousness, as postulated, denotes a self-contradictory relationship that both exists and does not exist at a given time. By employing such terms it is possible to achieve a sort of strained comprehension of certain phenomena but in doing so the reality upon which the phenomena are based, becomes distorted and almost totally misunderstood.

An instance of this is to be seen in some ideas concerning the nature of the Waking state that have received a wide exposition. They are to be attributed to an offshoot of the original Gurdjieff Institute, repudiated for many years but now having gained acceptability after the death of Gurdjieff himself. Like the religiosity that has accreted upon the same offshoot school, they are entirely incompatible with the Fourth Way represented by the original Institute.

These ideas, taken over bodily from the subjectivism of psychoanalysis, refer to a perfectly real situation that was the subject of an original Institute proposition. The fallacy involved is the result of an incorrectly subjective interpretation.

The error consists in the thesis that in the Waking state not just one 'I'-entity but many conflicting and contradictory 'I'-entities exist. But in the Waking state, as elsewhere, there can be only a single 'I'-entity involved; in this case its condition is that of I_0 but even in such a condition its conceptual postulation as an enduring and single entity is definitory of as much real existence as it possesses.

However, as we in the Waking state well know, we manifest contradictory personality patterns successively: sometimes we are honest, sometimes dishonest; on some occasions we are fair and impartial, on others unjustly unfair; at times we exhibit clear and rational thought process, and not long afterwards we are caught in some ridiculous error of logic. The misinterpretation of this circumstance is that it indicates a swarm of mutually opposing 'I'-entities, each struggling for authority, each gaining a brief ascendancy and each in turn being elbowed out and succeeded by one of the others. The idea is appropriated plainly from psychoanalysis and includes such vague analogies as multiple personalities, unconscious states of consciousness and similar irrational antitheses.

A proper analysis shows a very different picture. The 'I'-entity in its Waking condition of I_O is completely passive and cannot possibly manifest such activities as being fair or unfair, honest or dishonest, logical or illogical. These latter manifestations, and all others like them, are the activities of the organism, never of I_O.

But in the Waking state I_O, the purely passive registrar of organic event, continually identifies itself with the organism and thus must identify itself successively with every mutually contradictory organic manifestation as it arises in turn in the associated body. It is this identification with the organism that deludes I_O into the false belief that it itself is committing the contradictions that in fact comprise the successive organic events which it is registering only passively in its passive experience. Actually the 'I'-entity is no more committing these acts than it is controlling its passively registered thought processes, emotions or the other physical reactions of the body. The organism is performing the whole business, including the contradictions with which, like the rest, I_O automatically identifies itself.

In fact, to phantasy a whole horde of 'I'-entities constantly changing places like a party of dancers engaged in a quadrille is analogical subjectivism with a vengeance and indicates that the victim of such a concept is himself immersed in organic identification. It resembles the similar Ouspenskian exaggeration of introspective self-remembering which was once defined, perhaps not very seriously, as non-identification accompanied by delusions of grandeur. All such mistakes are typical of the Waking state which, to sane reflection, is a very queer condition indeed.

This, then, is the queerness of man in the Waking state. First, that in the place of an active, naturally coordinating consciousness he manifests a passively conscious mode which is accountable for his dazed, semi-conscious condition. Second, that such consciousness as he does manifest, is incomplete as well as passive. Third, that the result is the discordant, rather than the harmonious, functioning of his integrative mechanisms, which causes the three abnormal types of intellectual, emotional and practical man, all of them at the expense, both interior and exterior, of the other two. Another result is the inconsistent and contradictory behavior from which, because of automatic identification, arises the false belief in numerous opposing 'I'-entities.

In these circumstances it may no longer seem so astonishing (as at first it does) that the usual manifestation of the Waking state is one of accepting ignorantly a hodge-podge of false propositions, of being biased in crassly personal ways and of acting upon prejudiced misinformation. The dizzy, only partially conscious condition of the Waking state results in abnormal action, abnormal emotion and abnormal thought process, their sequence itself reversed from the natural order. In all of these judgments our standard has been the structural-functional mechanism, the human organism, which is accessible to our examination and whose characteristic design reflects and defines the human paradic.

Man's departure from the effectiveness of his designed organic functions is a measure of the abnormality of the Waking state in which it occurs. We have seen that consciousness (pure awareness irrespective of its object) represents the patterning factor in the complex of three primary forces that constitute a human being; and we have seen that the design of man demands that such pure awareness or consciousness *per se* be of an active kind. The last, in fact, must follow from the nature of any adequately patterning force.

On the other hand, an examination of human beings in the Waking state shows that their consciousness is not of an active but of a passive kind (mere registration). This circumstance results first in its incompleteness and then in the whole sequence of further abnormalities affecting the three primary categories of conscious content or experience. Such experience subsequently has drastic effects upon behavior, causing it to become of the abnormal sort actually manifested. But the passivity of consciousness is the chief defining characteristic of the Waking state.

In this state the 'I'-entity, manifesting a purely passive relationship to its organic sources of experience, is in the condition we have labelled as I_O. In other words, the 'I'-entity's existence in the Waking state, although real in a certain legitimate sense, is that of a postulate necessary in order to satisfy the rational requirements of other unquestionable aspects of reality. Apart from this the 'I'-entity can be said scarcely to exist at all or, rather, although its ultimate existence cannot be doubted rationally, its utter passivity easily raises such doubts in the absence of a rigorous analysis. The present standing of the Waking state thus is plain: in it the 'I'-entity, one of the basic factors or elements in the full economy of the human being, is always at the level of I_O.

This is the state in which credulity flourishes, in which transgressions are committed, in which high policy decisions are reached and wars are fought. This is the state in which our Public History is made—the History of Crime, as Ouspensky has called it. Strangely enough, almost all of us agree with that verdict, even while semiconsciously contributing to that history. From this we can appreciate not only that the Waking state itself is an abnormal condition or degree of consciousness but that by its nature it is bound to, and does, bring about the most abnormal results in private and public behavior.

Yet no easy reforms can cure this case. The problem of altering the effects is the problem of changing the conscious state from which those effects proceed. That problem is both subtle and difficult, as aforesaid; and it is always an individual problem in which success, though demanding the assistance of others, can be only individual, too. Upon the supposition that individual success is at least *possible*, we may next examine the different state of consciousness upon which it must rest.

REFERENCES IN THE TEXT OF CHAPTER V

1) *Dictionary of psychology*, ed. Warren, Houghton Mifflin Co., Boston, 1934.
2) Burr, H. S. and Associates. A list of publications by H. S. Burr and associates, 1916-1956; Section of Neuroanatomy, Yale University School of Medicine, 1957.
3) Gerard, R. W.   *Unresting cells*, Harper, N.Y., 1940: p. 154.
4) *Gould's medical dictionary*, ed. Brownlow, Blakiston Co., Philadelphia, 5th Edition, 1941.
5) Huxley, A.   *After many a summer dies the swan*, Harper, N.Y., 1939: pp. 309-310.
6) Wolfle, D.   Diversity of talent, *Amer. Psychologist*, August, 1960, 15: 535-545. (The Walter Van Dycke Bingham Memorial Lecture, 1960.)

chapter VI

AWAKENESS

IN REGARD TO THE STATE OF SLEEP we have voluminous physiological data referring to organic conditions and acquired by painstaking objective research performed upon subjects, both animal and human, who can be examined while in the Sleep state.

Except for AC and DC measurements contrasting Sleep and Waking conditions we have little data of the above kind upon Waking as a general state of the organism but this is chiefly because of a lack of interest in the matter and because in the usual case most data taken from subjects are procured while they are in the Waking state, this being accepted as their proper and ordinary condition. (1). From this it results that there is little discrimination between information relating to particular part-reactions and those data that refer to the general Waking state as such. But in regard to Awakeness we labor under even greater difficulties.

The chief obstacle is not in obtaining the relevant physiological information but in discovering the necessary subjects from whom to procure it. Supposing that we have a laboratory and its instrumentation at our disposal, where are we to find the human subjects from whom the findings may be taken? Manifestly it is impossible to assemble physiological data on the state of Awakeness unless we are able to secure subjects in that state, who may be examined objectively while they are in it. And where are we to discover them?

This question must be faced first of all and doubtless the reader himself will demand it. If we are to discuss Awakeness as a real state of consciousness, the reader is entitled to ask: does anyone at all exist in this alleged state? If so, how many people do so? For that matter, what about the writer himself? Do the statements to be made arise from his own experience or is he reporting only what someone else has told him? These are legitimate questions deserving of rational answers.

It was a requirement of the original Institute that one must maintain one's scepticism and that *no one* is entitled to make definite assertions of this character unless they are within his confirmed personal experience. It is from that point of view that the replies shall be given.

With one exception the writer has never encountered anyone of whom he felt assured that the latter was living permanently in a state of Awakeness. The exception was Gurdjieff himself. But because it is impossible for anyone to know or fully to understand another whose degree of being is upon a distinguishably higher level than his own, this statement cannot be more than a deductive judgment.

The grounds for the judgment rest simply upon common sense. The state of Awakeness is so different from that of Waking that one would naturally suppose and expect anyone in such a conscious state to exhibit a different level of manifestation than in the Waking state. The reference is not to marvels and wonders such as levitation and miracles but to the mode of living and the manner of contact with other persons, friendly, hostile or neutral. In these respects and many more Gurdjieff manifested himself in ways never elsewhere encountered by the writer, in ways so different from those of others that they constituted a plain and perceptible difference in level of existence upon his part. His famous reputation as an enigmatic rested largely upon this circumstance. He is the only person ever met by the writer who gave the indubitable impression that all his responses, mental, emotional and practical, were mutually *in balance* and thus the further impression that everyone else was out of step, but not this man himself. It is just what would be expected, though unpredictable, by a sophisticated Waking person when confronted by someone else in the state of Awakeness. So much for the judgment; of course no proof exists.

As to others, the writer feels convinced that his own instructor, Alfred Richard Orage, experienced the state of Awakness on many occasions but that he did not live in it permanently. However, he knew far too much about it to have gained his knowledge second-hand, merely from the reports of others. A few of the writer's pupils in this discipline also convinced him, by their questions and by their objectively tested reports, that they had experienced moments or more extended durations of Awakeness.

As for the writer himself, of course he knows that these experiences have occurred to him. They have occurred on occasions sufficiently numerous so that, if another were to happen right now, he would no longer feel so astounded and *bouleversé* as on early occasions when he, too, hastened for reassurance that he was not suffering from self-imposed delusions. An instance will be given later on.

But, with the exception of the writer, none of the above persons has ever been available for objective laboratory investigation and in his own case there has never been anyone available and sufficiently interested to act as investigator. Moreover in the writer's case periods of Awakeness have not been predictable to a degree permitting of laboratory research in the present sense.

For these reasons we are forced to go to the Gurdjieff Institute for our data upon the physiological conditions of the state of Awakeness, since it was the only modern organization that has investigated the problem in any accurate way. For of course we know that the organism is in different conditions in Waking than in Sleep and that it must be in even more dissimilar ones during Awakeness.

THE STATES OF HUMAN CONSCIOUSNESS

A partial description of the physiology of the state of Awakeness requires us to return again to the complex operations of organic food digestion. In this respect the situation in the Waking state will be recalled: the anabolic progress of the digestion of the oral food through its first three stages to the gaseous state, its confrontation with the absorbed gases of the nasal food at the level of the liver, its subsequent completion of its own anabolic octave through the genetic stage as a result of the foregoing mechanical shock, and the automatic progression of the air or nasal octave through the fiirst three steps of its digestion, ending with the production of electrical energy. Here the anabolic air octave must cease in the absence of external reinforcement but meantime the digestion of the oral food has furnished a full range of energies for the manifestation of mechanically passive man.

Up to this point nature has provided for the active assimilation of the two kinds of food intake but here the process stops, although just at this point, too, there is an abundance of the third category of food-substance proper to a normally functioning human being.

But in the absence of its active assimilation this third type of food will no more be digested and thus furnish its proper anabolic products than would our oral food if it merely lay passively in the mouth until it were drooled out again eventually. Anabolism is an active process but, whereas nature automatically provides for the active assimilation of the first two categories of food intake, nature does not do so in the case of the third category of food-substance. Only the man himself can do that and, since he does not actively digest this third form of his proper food, its fate is analogous to being drooled out of the organism without the production of any further anabolic transformations. Thus also it fails to provide the shock demanded for the further progression of the air octave of digestion, now stalled at its own third step of electrical energy-production.

In order to explain further this idea of electrical and similar energies serving, at their different anabolic stages, as forms of organic food, we must consider a series of propositions, as follows:

Proposition # 1: The human organism comprises three basic components, viz., its energies, its constituent entities, its electromagnetic field.

Proposition # 2: All of these three factors or components are mutually interacting but fully independent of each other, i.e., no one of them manufactures or creates either of the others. Organic phenomena take place due to their concurrent but independent activity.

Proposition # 3: The functioning of the organic field is simply and solely a patterning mediation.

Proposition # 4: The field does not create the constituent entities that are within it; instead, it controls and determines only their organization. Such entities, arising from sources quite different from that of the field, must find themselves within it before their manifestation can reflect the pattern of the field.

Proposition # 5: The field does not create the energies within its boundaries; instead, it only patterns their manifestation. Such energies, originating from sources altogether independent from the field, must find themselves within it before their manifestation can be patterned or organized by the field.

Corollary: Neither the entities nor the energies create the field; they merely permit the field to manifest its own properties of organization through them.

Proposition # 6: There is a magnetic field around nerve tracts during the conduction of nerve currents through them.

Proposition # 7: Magnetic fields are characterized by north and south poles and these north and south poles characterize the living cells that are within such magnetic fields.

Proposition # 8: If living cells are characterized by magnetic fields, then such cells contain or possess the attributes of what is called magnetism.

Proposition # 9: Electrical potential differences (whether or not across phase boundaries) also characterize electromagnetic fields but they are never the *sources* of electrical energy; instead, they constitute simply the evidence for the measurable presence of a field.

Proposition #10: Neither does the field generate any electrical energy, it only organizes or patterns such energy as is within it. Current flows from a higher to a lower potential (depending upon how we look at it) but, in order that this flow may take place, the current or the electrical energy must be there first, and its origin is other than from the field.

Proposition #11: The origin of the energies of the body is not from the electromagnetic organic field of the body but, instead, it is from the ingested food (which contains energies before it is ingested) and from its further transformations due to the anabolic processes of digestion.

Proposition #12: Since the body does possess magnetic and electrical energies, the origin of these, as well as of
most others, is from the ingested food and its
further transformations.

From these twelve propositions it is seen that the magnetism and
the electricity in the body are to be considered as the results of organic
anabolism. But it is now necessary to notice an energy-input to the
body *additional* to the above, although at first glance it is easy to confuse the two. This additional input constitutes the third form of
organic food and, in turn, it can be anabolized further.

The third form of natural food available to the human organism
has been called "impressions". The term is a perfectly correct one
but demands further explanation. If we consider a sensory impression, for example, this phenomenon comprises two aspects, the purely
neurological aspect of its history within the human body and, in addition, its experiential aspect when it is registered in the consciousness
of the 'I'-entity involved. In the present technical sense of the term it
becomes an impression — and consequently it becomes a food-source
— only when it is registered *actively* in the subject's consciousness; the
usual passive registration will fail to effect its availability as an organic
food. Therefore it is necessary to distinguish between a passive impression (the usual kind that does not serve as food) and an active impression (one registered actively in consciousness and thereby becomes an
anabolizable food, comparable to the oral and nasal varieties).

But the last statement has to be qualified further, for even a passive
(i.e., an unanabolizable) impression serves in some sort as an indis-
pensible form of food. Without oral food we can live for days, without
nasal food for minutes, but it has been calculated that, in the complete absence of passive sensory impressions, no human being can
survive beyond the duration of 1/30,000 second. This is because at
least passive impressions are demanded for survival, and they enter

[handwritten margin note:] bits or Logon Content.

[handwritten note at bottom:] Consciousness is a vitamin

the body at about 30,000 per second; thus there must be at least one every 1/30,000 second if the body is to continue to live. If, however, such impressions enter only passively, they will not permit of fully *human* living but merely of the kind of life experienced by animals.

Accordingly, the impressions of which we shall treat now in describing the third form of human food, will be the activated impressions which alone can serve the nutritional function. Our usual passive impressions will not be significant. But how can the latter be rendered active neurologically?

First we will trace the neurological history of the relevant impressions. To begin with, they enter the organism as energy manifestations. of various kinds — mechanical pressures, sound and light waves of different frequencies, chemical stimuli to the taste buds in the mouth or to the nasal receptors, and so on. These energies may be both of external and of internal origin but then they are transformed immediately by the organism: the passively stimulated receptors react actively upon their associated afferent (sensory) nerves, setting up electrical nerve impulse propagations that pass sometimes through the thalamus to the cerebral arrival platforms and sometimes directly to similar destinations. This whole mass of sensory nerve impulse groups then is integrated within the cerebrum with the neural activities proceeding there. Up to this point we are dealing entirely with the usual passive impressions, characteristic of the ordinary Waking and Sleep states, which are registered passively and only in part by the 'I'-entity in its condition of I_0.

But that is not the end of the story, for the cerebrum is not the end of the line. In turn it discharges vast numbers of nerve impulses further, about 33 per cent to the motor centers for the responses of the organism to the environmental situation, about 66 per cent directly to the central cerebellum, and perhaps 1 per cent or less from the inner ear through the outlying portions of the cerebellum to serve the equilibritory reflexes of the muscles. Thus we are being generous if we concede that 34 per cent of the tremendous cerebral output is utilized by the organism. The 66 per cent direct stimulation to the cerebellum vanishes; the chief cerebellar lobes comprise so-called "silent" areas that are nonfunctional, so far as can be ascertained.

As to the vestibular system "no definite (outward) connections to cortical denters are indicated. . . . There are possible pathways to the thalamus from the cerebellar cortex through the dentate nucleus and the brachium conjunctivum" but these are "inconspicuous and of questionable significance." (3). The discharge from this part of the cerebellum to the lower motor neurones takes place through the red nucleus and the rubrospinal tract from the dentate nucleus in the roof of the fourth ventricle.

Synergy is a concept of the effect produced by the *spinal* reflexes through the cerebellum. It is asserted to bring about the coordination of separate motor innervations into a complex whole and thus the production of smoothly functioning movements from combinations of disparate muscular stimulations. The timing of the neural impulse discharge to peripheral muscles is suggested as a synergic function by recent researches, and such a mechanism must take effect through a cerebellar influence upon the final common motor pathways.

Synergy is plainly an integrative effect brought to bear upon the efferent arc of the total response system. And just why this additional integration is required on the efferent side when simple synaptic integration is sufficient over the afferent and central portions of the arc, is not readily apparent. But so far as is now ascertained, these synergic phenomena seem to be the case. However, they do not involve the major portion of the cerebellum, the middle lobes and their adjuncts, which remain nonfunctional on present evidence. In fact the removal of most of the cerebellum, experimentally, surgically, or as a result of inherited defect, brings about no loss of integrative function upon present findings; and this again evidences the present lack of function of the main portions of the cerebellum.

This is an astounding circumstance, affecting one of the chief neurological systems of the body, and for years it has astounded every competent neurologist who has thought about it seriously. The cerebral exits are the last points of the afferent and central arcs, whereafter the organic activity becomes that of the efferent arc. And what happens at this location to roughly two-thirds of the results of the entire afferent input to the body? Does it just vanish? Or is its fate equivalent to being drooled out of the organism nonfunctionally and impotently? Our answer to the last question is affirmative.

This contemporary nonfunctional aspect of the cerebellum adds much weight to the hypothesis of the presence but non-use of the third category of food supply just at the cerebellar point where the air octave of digestion is stalled at the electrical stage. The great input to the cerebellum is electrical; it consists of millions of nerve impulse groups entering within a very short period of time, the conduction of such nerve impulses is by means of action currents over the cortico-ponto-cerebellar tract, and action currents are electric currents.

Thus it appears that there is a constant supply of this form of energy to the cerebellum from the outlying parts of the nervous system but that this energy vanishes completely or almost completely, since the anabolic products of the oral and nasal octaves of digestion are quite sufficient to take care of the vestibular or equilibritory reflexes and the synergic influence, which now comprise the only known cerebellar functions.

The contention here is that this constant electrical supply is, as it were, drooled out non-functionally because it is not assimilated *actively* at its points of usable entry, namely at the cerebellar terminus of the cortico-ponto-cerebellar tract. Were it there to be assimilated actively, i.e., were it to be digested as the oral and nasal categories of food-substances are digested, the first effect would be to reinforce the air octave of anabolism, thus permitting it to complete its own sevenfold progression, and the second effect would be the completion by the impressions octave of its own first three steps of anabolism. There would then be available in the organism a great multiplication of energies as compared with the present situation, as will be seen from the tables below:

Oral Food   *Nasal Food*   *Neural Food*

		si
		la
	si	sol
	la	fa
si genetic	sol	mi
la cardiac	fa	re
sol electrical	mi electrical	do (electrical)
fa magnetic	re magnetic	(shock)
mi gaseous	do gaseous	
re liquid		
do solid		

(shock — between Oral magnetic/gaseous)

Table 1: Present Situation

Oral Food   *Nasal Food*   *Neural Food*

		si
		la
	si nectareous	sol
	la ambrosial	fa
si genetic	sol genetic	mi genetic
la cardiac	fa cardiac	re cardiac
	first conscious shock	
sol electrical	mi electrical	do electrical
fa magnetic	re magnetic	
mechanical shock		
mi gaseous	do gaseous	
re liquid		
do solid		

Table 2: Hypothetical Situation

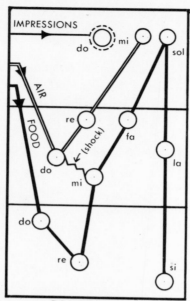

DIAGRAM III

Diagram of Digestion Stages in Ordinary Man

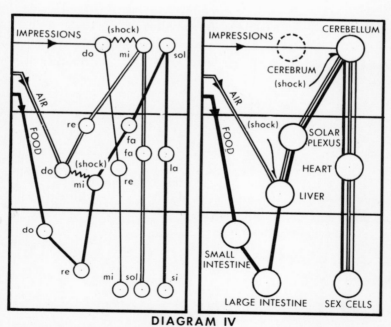

DIAGRAM IV

Diagrams of Digestion Stages after Second (conscious) shock

In the first situation only two sources of electrical energy are present and only one source of cardiac and genetic energies. In the second situation there are present not only three sources of electrical energy but three sources of cardiac and genetic energies as well. In addition there are two further forms of energy from the complete anabolism of the nasal food. At present we have no accurate terms for these but the ancient Greeks gave them two somewhat fanciful names. The writer professes to have no more reliable knowledge than does the reader as to the physical states of these last two alleged forms of energy; but they must definitely be implied from the nature of these analytical tables.

The question then arises as to the manner in which the third category of food-substances is to be assimilated actively. Since nature will not do it for us, we ourselves must initiate this assimilative activity and the details of the process already have been given in the earlier chapter dealing with the activation of consciousness. It is precisely by transforming a passive registration into an active observation of our sensations and our gross behavior that the electroneural sources of energy constantly present at the cerebellar location in the nervous system can begin to be assimilated actively and thus commence their own anabolism. Simultaneously they reinforce the nasal food digestion for its ultimate completion.

As explained previously, any genuine laboratory confirmation of the above statements must be lacking today, not only because of an absence of academic interest in the matter but, more unfortunately, because of the absence of any properly qualified subjects whose examination could be expected to yield the desired information. But at this point of the discussion the argument from the physiological to the psychological is both rational and simple, and now can be adduced.

Since we have known for a long time that two-thirds of the large neural output from the cerebral cortex is projected directly upon the

Pineal gland in brain produces a sex hormone

cerebellum, it is clear that there is an abundance of this form of energy taken in by the latter organ.

Let us be specific. The vestibular reflexes originate in the semi-circular canals of the inner ear and are directed to the cerebellar flocculus, nodulus, lingula and uvula, thence downwards through the rubrospinal tract. This system mediates equilibrium. Generally stated, the spinal reflex impulses come in through the spinocerebellar tracts, pass through the culmen, biventral lobule, pyramis, tonsilla and central lobule, and descend through the dentatorubral and rubro-spinal fibers, thus mediating synergy. These two systems are functional but they comprise only the lesser portions of the cerebellum.

The superior and inferior lobes, the declive, the folium and the tuber make up the major portion of the cerebellum and it is by these that the great input from the cerebrum is received. They comprise the "silent" or non-functional areas of the cerebellum, upon which the energies of the cerebral cortex impinge through the cortico-ponto-cerebellar tract. They are the terminal points of this projection of energy input.

But we know that the operation is a purely mechanical one, that no assimilative process occurs here comparable to the anabolic diges-tion of our oral food in the gastrointestinal tract or to that of the absorbed gases from the inhaled air when they reach the liver through the pulmonary circulation.

However, the cerebellar cortex is generally of like kind to the cere-bral cortex, possessing a threefold instead of a sevenfold cytoarchi-tecture, having many association or correlation arcs connecting its various regions and even possessing centers of functional localization whose mediations are not too well defined, since at present the organ appears to be mainly non-functional except for its reflex vestibular and synergic reactions.

From all of these ascertained facts it is a reasonable assumption that, just as portions of the cerebral cortex furnish the raw material for the subjective experience of the 'I'-entity, so comparable regions of the cerebellar cortex might be expected to furnish the same. But in addition to these resemblances there are distinctions to be noted. The cerebellar cortex, unlike the cerebral, is uniform, suggesting a uniform functional mediation. Moreover, the energies received by the cerebral cortex in the form of neural impulses projected upon it from the receptor system and the basal ganglia are mediated as a result of the active anabolic processes previously performed by the digestive operations of the organism, for these electrical energies, like all others, are obviously the digestive result of the body's food intake, although stimulated anew by the afferent input to the body. But the cerebral output to the cerebellum, already having fulfilled its response potentialities in the cerebrum, is now in the condition only of raw electrical supply and for that reason now again can be subjected to further anabolism.

It is also to be noted, as in the cases of all other energies anabolized within the organism, that a portion of the electrical output from the cerebrum is used for current organic purposes and that another (larger) portion is available for further digestion. The currently used portion is projected upon the motor centers from the cerebral cortex, while an additional small amount goes to the minor mechanisms of the cerebellum where it takes part in the current vestibular reflexes, synergy being mediated by a spinal, not a cerebral, input to the cerebellum.

But the major portion of the cerebral output to the cerebellum is over the cortico-ponto-cerebellar tract. This latter output, although non-functional at present, constitutes the energies of electrical character which are available potentially for further organic anabolism at the indicated cerebellar level. But it is at this level, too, that the electrical energies already present have been anabolized previously. Thus the cerebral output to the same level can serve potentially as a reinforcement for the nasal digestive stage which at this point has come to a stop at its third step of electrical production.

At this juncture the selected (cerebellar) localization of the *new* digestive process is bound to be questioned. Nerve impulse conduction, it will be said, is the same throughout the organism; why, then, make an exception of the cortico-ponto-cerebellar tract and imply that these nerve impulse groups are different from any others? Why should they constitute potential neural food intake, if quite similar nerve impulse groups elsewhere do not do so?

Of course this rebuttal is not entirely cogent. Why, one may also ask, is the frontothalamic tract so important for the crucial functions it mediates, when its nerve impulse conduction is no different from the same sort of conduction elsewhere? Naturally the reason for its importance lies in the origin and the terminus of what is conducted. The same answer could be given in the cerebro-cerebellar case. But there are other reasons, too. One is that these impulses may constitute potential neural food intake because nothing else happens to them at the loci of the chief cerebellar lobes where they are received. In this respect, certainly, they are distinguishable from almost all other conduction in the body.

The input received by the cerebral cortex is there transformed into the raw material of mental and sensory experience, just as the basal gangliar input is transformed into the raw material of motational experience. But here we have a very large input to one of the chief organs of the head brain system and it produces no discernible effect whatever, a conclusion reinforced by the effect of excision, already mentioned. Surely the design itself of this portion of the nervous system must convince us that some potential effect is to be expected to take place at this location.

Another reason is that the input is not only large but concentrated at the specified location. Likewise it consists of the most complexly integrated impulse series in the organism, for the cerebral output comes directly from the correlation centers where the utmost degree of integration has taken place. It is also constant, for the cerebral output to the cerebellum does not cease even in the Sleep state.

When we recognize that this large, highly integrated and highly concentrated stream of neural electrical energy has no ascertainable result whatever at its identified terminus, it is no longer gratuitous to attribute the lack of result to an absence of required activity at this locus or to speak of the energy there present as being drooled out of the organism impotently. We know that at this location no organic process of anabolism takes place and our argument is that it is just this absence of activity which renders the input nonfunctional at the mentioned point.

In order to perform any further function this cerebellar intake must once more be anabolized in its turn, and this is precisely what nature does not do for us. Hence the psychological part of the argument: that the third anabolic process now lacking at the cerebellar level must be initiated by the subject himself and that this can be done only by his own activity *vis à vis* the entering energy, namely by his being aware actively of what the entering energy represents — the sum total of all the current responses, sensory, emotional and mental and their integrations, which stand for his concomitant subjective experience.

By the nature of the case such activity can be only conscious in kind and this liveliness of consciousness is exactly what earlier we have called its activation. The gradual steps by which such activation can be inaugurated, already have been described.

It will now be asked how the mere awareness of the cerebral events and what they represent, can possibly activate these nervous impulses, thus causing the cerebellar input to undergo further anabolic transformation at that level.

So far as can be ascertained, this phenomenon is comparable to that of catalysis of a specific kind. Catalysis in the strictest sense is the occurrence of a reaction between two or more elements in the presence of a third or separate element which itself takes no part in the reaction but in whose absence no reaction will occur. The analogy here is obvious: the mentioned direct awareness must consist by definition in a non-identified observation and thus it takes no part in the organic reactions observed. But the resemblance is closer than that; it is not an analogy but a correspondence. For we know that certain phenomena can occur only in the presence of the catalyst which we call light and that they refuse to take place when surrounded by darkness. Apparently the awareness involved here has an effect similar to light upon the energy transformations at the cerebellar locus, causing them to ensue as they cannot do in the absence of the observational activity.

About such an effect there is nothing any more mystical than there is about catalysis in general. The latter is not very clearly understood in chemical terms and so neither can the present phenomenon be described accurately in minute detail. But both events are of a purely physical kind, as is never doubted in the former case.

The physiological results of such activation have been set forth theoretically in the last table above, showing the great increase in organic energies present for use in the body under the conditions of an active (rather than a passive) relation between the subjective entity and the neural material upon which its experience rests.

This activity of the subjective factor or 'I'-entity will be focussed upon the cerebral loci of the experiential raw material, namely upon the final arrival platforms in the case of sensations and upon the cerebral correlation centers in the case of the bodily images representing our gross physical behavior. But the *effect* of such activity will be registered at the cerebellar lobes upon which this now activated cerebral output impinges.

Thus an expected result of the operation of an active consciousness would consist in the functional activation of the chief cerebellar lobes.

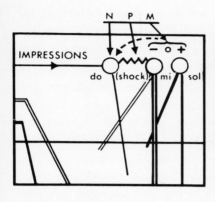
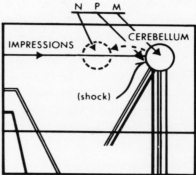

+ = positive factor
− = negative factor
O = neutralizing factor

M: designates derivation of energy
N: designates application of energy
P: designates effective result

DIAGRAM V
Detail of second (conscious) shock

In passive conditions these mediate nothing; but the functions of the minor portions of the cerebellum that account for the vestibular reflexes and the phenomenon of synergy, permit us to surmise that the lobar functions may be those of balance and coordination also.

In that case they might well fulfill the mediation alleged for them theoretically, namely the general regulation of the body's sensory, emotional and mental responses so that they then would manifest in a balanced manner, integrated into harmonious unit responses of the whole organism. It may even be supposed that, with the cerebellum in complete functional operation, the subdivisions of such unit responses might come into a paradic relation with each other, reversing their present abnormal sequence and manifesting the proper relationship to each other of mental, emotional and practical reactions successively, thus comprising a complete unit response conforming to the genuine human design.

We have been discussing a general proposition of the original Gurdjieff Institute and formulating it in contemporary scientific terms. But the exposition has been of some length and it may be well to summarize its main points:

The energies of the body are recruited from the food intake of the body and its subsequent anabolism.

Among these are the electrical energies used by the organism.

Like all other energies, a part of the electrical energy is used in the current operations of the body and another part is available for further anabolism.

As to the electrical energy present in the cerebrum these two portions, generally speaking, are respectively the output from the cerebral centers to the motor centers and the similar output to the cerebellum.

At present the latter is not subjected to further anabolism and thus is wasted, rendering the major portion of the cerebellum nonfunctional.

This situation may be reversed by the activity of the 'I'-entity in observing directly the current sensory and behavioral phenomena of the associated organism.

Such activity on the part of the subjective entity will be directed upon the relevant cerebral centers, thus activating the cerebral output to the cerebellar lobes.

This activated cerebellar input will render the cerebellum fully functional and create a then balanced operation of the total organism. Q.E.D.

At the present time all this must remain mostly theoretical; the evidence existing in favor of the contentions of the current chapter comes mainly from the subjective side of the question. This must be accepted, of course, with the proper reservations applicable to all subjective testimony but nonetheless the affirmations of competent witnesses do, and ought to, carry some weight when it is sought to reach impartial judgments. This evidence will relate to the conscious state of Awakeness and to the information gathered about it by those who have experienced it confirmably, at least in part or for relatively short periods.

This state of consciousness can be experienced only deliberately, as a result of prolonged conscious effort upon our part. Therefore it does not form a part of our ordinary common experience and its description in subjective terms will be unfamiliar to the reader. For this reason we will preface the discussion by stating certain premises.

To start with, let us premise that we are all in the Sleep state at some given time and that we wish to communicate with each other under those conditions. Of course that is impossible but assuming that it could be done (for the sake of the analogy to follow), let us consider the problem of how one who is only temporarily asleep, could describe to his companion, who has never been in any other state than that of Sleep, the conditions that are to be experienced in the Waking state. Plainly this would be a most difficult undertaking because the recipient of the information would have at his command none of the verbal expressions or even the concepts required for his understanding of the information to be conveyed.

The problem is identical with that which arises when it is desired to acquaint a person who has had no experience beyond the Waking state, with some idea of the experiences to be encountered in the state of Awakeness. Our verbal terms and labels have all developed from our Waking experiences and this origin renders them entirely inadequate as symbols of communication in respect of conditions upon a level as different from Waking as is the latter from Sleep. Thus it is to be understood that some of the formulations of this chapter can consist only of hints and suggestions, drawn from Waking experience, whereby it is sought to convey some rational idea of the nature of the conscious state of Awakeness.

This does not mean that there is anything mystical or supernatural about Awakeness. To the constant sleeper any description of Waking must appear strange and bizarre but we know perfectly well that

Waking, while full of daydreams and phantasies, is in no way a mystical state. Neither is Awakeness; but we cannot fail to recognize that its description, to one who has never experienced it, must seem strange and bizarre in certain respects.

All of us realize that external reality appears very differently when one is awake than it does when one is asleep. The steam radiator, going on automatically early in the morning, may affect our current dreams but we are not then in a position to attribute the alteration of the temperature to the heating system of the house. When awake, on the other hand, we attribute the change to the radiator so immediately that it passes with almost no conscious thought process at all. This is not true in early childhood, however; it results from a long acquaintance with our external surroundings and the ways in which they operate. Comparable alterations in our perceptions of external reality are to be expected in the state of Awakeness but to one who experiences a few moments of that state for the first time, they naturally will be as inexplicable as are the impressions of a naive, inexperienced child.

This is one of the reasons that companions are necessary upon such a path. When one first perceives totally novel and unexpected aspects of the external world, it is very reassuring to discover an entirely sane friend who has experienced the same thing. Do-you-see-what-I-see is a frequent demand posed by those who have reached a certain stage in the discipline. It is an encouraging question; it shows that they are accomplishing something.

Another point must be noticed about Awakeness. One remains the same entity whether asleep or awake, and one still remains the same whether awake or self-awakened. Because of the initial strangeness of Awakeness even this obvious circumstance is doubted sometimes by timid students and here again they stand in need of assistance from those more matured in the discipline. To be sure, these are minor matters and much more serious crises are bound to occur. It is another reason that the technique of activating the consciousness should never to be practiced without the most competent supervision or without the companionship of others at approximately the same stage as oneself.

Still another aspect of general states of consciousness is to be remarked. Although only in light sleep do we occasionally know that we are dreaming and thus currently in the Sleep state, everyone always knows that he is in the Waking state when in fact he does wake up. It is the same with the state of Awakeness. When it is entered, there is no doubt at all upon the part of the experiencer that a distinguishable state of consciousness has been attained.

Moreover, there is no doubt about the advantage of having done so. The periodical need for rest aside, almost everyone recognizes that it is better to be awake than asleep. This same instinctive value-standard applies in the same way to Awakeness as contrasted to Waking. No one who has ever experienced the former, can doubt its superiority over the Waking state in terms of conscious clarity and intensity or in those of his own human paradic.

Examples are always illustrative and, although the writer hesitates to obtrude personally upon the discussion, it may interest the reader to hear of two instances of the experience of Awakeness. These were very early ones (none of them are ever forgotten) and all of them have occurred only after prolonged efforts in the discipline that has been named as the activation of consciousness. They have happened as a result of those efforts but they have happened unexpectedly, which implies, first, that they were not instances of self-hypnosis due to anticipation and, second, that the writer is not as yet in sufficient control of his consciousness to be able to enter or to leave the state of Awakeness at will.

These occasions always occurred in the most prosaic circumstances, which was one of the intentions and purposes of the instructions as given by Orage. The first of them took place upon the platform of a commuters' railway station in New Jersey as the writer walked along it to take a coming train to New York late one sunny morning. On the platform there were several small housings for freight elevators, newsstands and so on, constructed of dun-colored bricks. He was emotionally at ease, planning unhurriedly the schedule of his various calls in the city and simultaneously attempting to be aware, actively and impartially, of the movements of his body's walking and actively to be conscious at the same time of all the auditory sensations arising through his ears.

Suddenly the entire aspect of the surroundings changed. The whole atmosphere seemed strangely vitalized and abruptly the few other persons on the platform took on an appearance hardly more important or significant than that of the doorknobs at the entrance of the passengers' waiting room. But the most extraordinary alteration was that of the dun-colored bricks. They remained, naturally, dun-colored bricks, for there was no concomitant sensory illusion in the experience. But all at once they appeared to be tremendously alive; without manifesting any exterior motion they seemed to be seething almost joyously inside and gave the distinct impression that in their own degree they were living actively and liking it. This impression so struck the writer that he remained staring at them for some minutes, until the train arrived and it was necessary for him to mount the steps and enter a car.

An interesting footnote to the experience is that the outstanding impressions accompanying the state of Awakeness apparently were unrelated to the efforts immediately preceding them. It was the bricks that stood out predominantly in the experience and these were chiefly *seen,* although there was more in the impression than visual perception. But there was certainly no auditory component nor any further sense of automatic muscular coordination. In the astonishment of the occurrence both of those efforts ceased but all of the environment remained perfectly real, if somewhat surprising, and with the arrival of the train and the necessity to board it the degree of consciousness relapsed to that of the ordinary Waking state. This, in fact, was because the efforts had ceased; had they continued, so would the conscious degree have done.

Another occasion took place at the terminus of this railroad at Hoboken on a different afternoon when the writer was returning home from New York. This time he was tired, though not greatly fatigued, and walked out onto the concourse from which the platforms to the trains led away. Again he had been making strenuous efforts in the mentioned discipline. It was later than the rush hour but there was still a considerable number of people proceeding to their various destinations.

Once more the scene altered unexpectedly and with a startling abruptness, as if one stage set had been substituted instantly for another. But now it was chiefly the other people who held the focus of attention. They looked dead, really dead. One expected to see signs of decay but of course there were none. What one did see was stark unconsciousness, scores of marionettes not self-propelled but moved by some force alien to themselves, proceeding along their automatic trails mechanically and without purpose. Some of the mouths were open and they looked like holes in cardboard boxes. The faces were blankly empty; even those upon which otherwise some expression would have been noticeable, had been drained of any significance and one saw that those expressions were unrelated to the entities that wore them. For the first time the concept of the zombie became credible.

The contrast between the emotional impacts of these two experiences was considerable. In the first instance there had been a this-is-right feeling; this is how it should be and thank God it is. In the second a very strange emotion accompanied the other impressions. It was a compound of contempt and pity; but it was not these two together, either simultaneously or successively. It was a hitherto unexperienced integration of the two for which no adequate term exists in our present vocabulary. For many years the writer had felt only contempt for the subhumans who so unpleasantly resemble himself, but this was not at all that sort of contempt. The amalgam changed the nature both of contempt and of pity, so that they no longer could be likened to their previous exemplifications. Perhaps it was some minor degree of what Orage used to call compassion, for in genuine compassion there is no hint or element of sentimentality or of that false kindliness that masquerades as altruism. True compassion is as cold as ice. Whatever this was, it brought a brand new experience to the writer.

These experiences, if described to the psychiatrist, no doubt would be labelled as hallucinatory. But anyone who has perceived a mirage and then has identified it as such, usually can recognize mirages thereafter. Hallucinations also are brought about often deliberately (for experimental purposes) in the psychological laboratory and the writer has a long personal experience with these, obtained during studies in physiological psychology. But the taste of the experiences just narrated is utterly different from hallucination and is distinguishable therefrom readily.

When the assertion of hallucination is made by someone who has never experienced the state of Awakeness, it resembles the supposedly similar assertion of a sleeper regarding Waking experiences theoretically described to him. Because the latter quite naturally cannot recognize them himself, he assumes them to be unreal whereas, if on his own part he wakes up, his opinion is changed very quickly.

The flavor of a real, as contrasted to a false, experience is difficult to describe but nonetheless it is recognizable when it takes place. The modern physicist well knows that such things as bricks are seething inside; the amount of molecular, atomic and electronic movement is tremendous. Ordinarily we have no perception of those phenomena but, if we should chance to obtain some impression of them, why label the experience as hallucination when in fact it corresponds quite faithfully to otherwise ascertained fact?

Other critics may say that experiences such as those related above are not unusual and thus do not indicate any basic alteration of consciousness. For example, as regards the second instance (in respect of an unusual view of a crowd of people) a small minority already considers ordinary persons *en masse* to be contemptible and will frequently find occasions upon which they appear so. This group will point to numerous persons in a crowd and declare that the dazedly unconscious appearance of such persons demonstrates the view, really the theory, which they hold. In this case the sensory impression triggers the associated theory already held and the comment, unless suppressed by convention or otherwise, follows automatically. Primarily the whole response is a thought-process reaction, depending upon a form of reasoning.

But the mentioned experiences of Awakeness include no thought-process whatever; that comes only afterward. The direct impression of the abnormality of the people observed is very different from any hypothesis about them, neither does it imply nor derive from any previously adopted theory. When the experience occurs, one is not looking for abnormality nor is one seeking evidences of a theory which may or may not be held by the subject of the experience. The seen abnormality comes as a shock, not as any kind of confirmation, and the indubitable difference is that no thought-process is involved at the time. Another distinction, of course, lies in the totally different emotional responses evoked, the first of self-satisfaction at a confirmation achieved, the second of an emotion entirely novel, at least to this writer. (2). The effect is much the same as would be produced by a sudden confrontation with a monstrous tree, hitherto unexperienced, bearing grotesquely malformed fruit.

Such experiences as the above, written out in our inefficient verbal symbols, may appear to be singularly unimpressive. But they are not. Several of them cannot fail to furnish one with the conviction that customarily we do live in something very like Waking dream and that in reality we are surrounded by an environment quite different from that which we perceive ordinarily.

Naturally none of this is designed to persuade the reader that the state of Awakeness is a genuine one, more objective in its character-istics than the Waking state. He can discover that only for himself. The above anecdotes are offered simply to appease his curiosity and to suggest that the Awakeness state, postulationally existing, is a form neither of hypnosis nor of phantasy if actually experienced.

Reports of this kind naturally were of frequent occurrence from the Institute pupils who were undergoing the mentioned discipline and of course it was necessary to check such reports against the possibility that they represented instances of fanciful imagination rather than correct realizations, actually experienced. There were at least two bases for such confirmations.

First, there was the comparability of the experiences of different pupils. If a given subject's constatations resembled those of others at the same stage of the discipline, there was the preliminary likelihood that what they were experiencing, was not due to personal idiosyncrasy or to personal self-hypnosis or to personal credulity concerning what they may have happened to hear during their instruction, for predic-tions of this kind never were made deliberately. But no two persons in the Waking state have exactly the same impressions nor can this be expected in the state of Awakeness, so that comparability cannot be the equivalent of identity. Nonetheless, there are common sense standards of comparability and in practice it was very easy to dis-tinguish the genuine experience from the phantastic self-illusion. Those who suffered from the latter, were instructed at once to desist from these efforts.

Second, with a considerable history behind it and with a number of instructors who themselves had already gone through the process, the Institute had at its command not only a practical knowledge of what is to be expected in the usual case of the pupil first introduced to this technique but a detailed theoretical background from which to predict what ought (and what ought not) to be the proper responses of naive persons having their first minor contacts with a conscious state beyond the Waking one.

By no means all the responses of this kind were correct and proper ones. Some were plainly unhinged, and in such cases the task of the instructor became an exacting undertaking. But of course the role of the Institute was not that of this book, namely the formulation of knowledge, but instead it was the development and training of selected individuals so that they could acquire a fully human status. A preliminary condition is the attainment of the conscious state of Awakeness.

In this connection it must be said that the technique of activating the consciousness, so prominent in the present discussion, was only a part of the full Institute discipline for the accomplishment of its purposes. Even in the early stages of the complete discipline there were additional steps called Participation and Experiment, and there were also further techniques, which we do not intend to describe here. The present work is concerned solely with the formulation of the states of consciousness possible for human beings and it does not treat of the means whereby they may be experienced except in illustration or explanation of the main thesis. In this chapter the nature of Awakeness, not its attainment, is the theme.

But the state of Awakeness is a very crucial one in respect of the total human economy and especially in regard to the subjective factor, the 'I'-entity. In this state the subjective factor for the first time assumes a degree of real objectivity, that is, the 'I'-entity becomes genuinely objective in its own right and no longer is real only as a necessary postulation from other aspects of reality. In other words, when I_0 alters to "I", it becomes a thing, not a postulate.

This is a most difficult proposition to clarify without going into parachemistry, paraphysics and the like, which we wish to avoid here.

In the Waking state the 'I'-entity exists as I_0 and basically I_0 is a concept, a concept demanded by the nature of reality, to be sure, but possessing no more reality than that, or in any case very little more.

This is because I_0 is completely passive, the mere registrar of what is happening to the organism associated with it as the first or positive factor in the full human economy. This passivity and the resulting lack of a separate reality are largely responsible for the circumstance that I_0 customarily identifies itself with the positively active factor related to it, namely with the organism. But even in the face of the technique of self-remembering or non-identification I_0 still remains conceptual and only when the activity of awareness is directed upon the behavior of the organism, does the first possibility of objectivity appear in relation to the 'I'-entity. When I_0 has become "I", then "I" is actually *doing* something; it is doing something that the organism cannot do and that which performs an action inherent in and to itself, must have a comparable degree of real objectivity.

As the conception of the embryo is hidden in the womb of the mother, so is the concept, I_0, hidden in the organism. It is with birth that a new member of the population appears and it is when I_0 has become "I" that for the first time the 'I'-entity can be said to be real in an objective sense. The establishment of the 'I'-entity as a separate integer in the whole economy comes with its activity, not with its mere conception. An active awareness in the previously defined sense demonstrates an active 'I'-entity, because no other factor can manifest that activity; and an active 'I'-entity is *ipso facto* an objectively real 'I'-entity. Concepts can *do* nothing; when something is done actively, there is an objective entity doing it.

In the state of Awakeness "I" manifests an active awareness of the organic phenomena with which it is associated. These phenomena cannot observe themselves, but "I" can observe them. The activity begins as described previously but naturally the technique is carried much farther, to behavior sequences, habits, experimental situations, until eventually an activity of consciousness is established that must inaugurate a conscious state far beyond Waking, which here we have called Awakeness.

If the practical possibility of this alteration, and especially its reference to the condition of the 'I'-entity, have been suggested, we now may consider the fourth state of consciousness allegedly possible for human beings.

REFERENCES IN THE TEXT OF CHAPTER VI.

1) *Dictionary of psychology,* ed. Warren, Houghton Mifflin Company, Boston, 1934. Page 294.

2) Ouspensky, P.   *In search of the miraculous,* Kegan Paul, Trench, Trubner, London, and Harcourt Brace, N.Y., 1949; p. 265.

3) Rasmussen, A.T. *The principal nervous pathways,* MacMillan Company, N.Y., 1941; p. 22.

chapter VII

OBJECTIVE CONSCIOUSNESS

WITH REGARD TO this state of consciousness we are on much less
secure ground than we have occupied so far. The writer certainly
has had no personal experience of it nor has he ever met anyone who
gave him reason to suppose that the latter had done so, either. We are
therefore dealing with what, for us, must be a hypothetical condition;
but the reports of it have been so widespread, and indeed so continuous throughout man's known history, that we must assume this state
to have the reality of actual occurrence. So many men in such different
civilizations and under the conditions of so widely varying cultures
scarcely could have given such serious accounts of it if it had no
existence at all outside their quite various imaginations.

We have distinguished earlier between the correct or paradic state
of Objective Consciousness and its abnormal counterpart, which goes
under the modern name of Cosmic Consciousness. Many books have
been written about the latter by those who claim to have experienced
it but the descriptions there given are not very intelligible. Aside from
their vagueness they are often mutually contradictory in addition,
and little can be learned from them beyond the indubitable impression that they are the result of peculiar and unnatural conditions
experienced haphazardly by those who have undergone them.

It is the suggestion here that all this comes about because the subjective entity involved in these experiences is the 'I'-entity in its condition of I_O, which is characteristic of the Waking state. The Waking state itself is one of light hypnosis in which the 'I'-entity identifies itself with the organism with which it is associated, with the consequence that this degree of consciousness is already clouded and unclear. When the highest degree of consciousness is entered directly from the Waking state, therefore, the vagueness and obscurity of the preceding condition is carried over to the succeeding one and the realizations of those who have recovered from a spell of Cosmic Consciousness and attempt to tell us of it, are scarcely intelligible at all.

They cannot fail to remind us of those other peculiar manifestations known as intuition, telepathy and clairvoyance. No doubt—or so we are told—all of these are the normal attributes of fully developed human beings but, when manifested prematurely by those who are not as yet fitted for their proper exercise, they must be uncontrolled and distorted in their functioning. It is as if we found a child of six or seven years successfully conducting the campaigns of Napoleon: we know that he cannot understand what he is doing and, although we are unable properly to blame him for such a capability, we assuredly do not envy him the possession of so freakish an attribute.

It is the same with Cosmic Consciousness which, entered from the Waking state, is basically a pathological condition and generates many kinds of delusions. An example is the statement of Eriksen, although he cannot be called a mystic in the genuine sense: "The predominance of life is generally connected with a lowering of consciousness and the predominance of the latter with a weakening of life." (8). Nothing could be farther from the case for, in fact, the greater the degree of consciousness, the greater the degree of life. Indeed it could be said, if we understand the sense in which Eriksen employs the term, life, that consciousness *is* life.

Among those who have sought to acquaint us with their meaning of Cosmic Consciousness Bucke has been as literate as any. (1). He divides the states or degrees of consciousness into four: Absence of Consciousness, Simple Consciousness, Self Conciousness and Cosmic Consciousness. Self Consciousness in his sense involves the confusion of consciousness with thought process; it rests upon a multiplicity of concepts and is based upon the introspective criterion that in this condition a man not only knows something but "knows that he knows it." (2). Such introspection is a Waking state activity and what we have called the Waking state is what Bucke calls Self Consciousness. It is, he says, from this last condition that the state Cosmic Consciousness is to be entered.

According to his description of it Cosmic Consciousness is a somewhat peculiar condition, to say the least of it. In it one becomes "insensible to surrounding objects," as in the case of Socrates (3); in other cases "the mind becomes a blank." There then occur various typical hallucinations, such as that of "Christ on the cross" (4) or the approach of a "six-winged seraph," and so on. In this condition elevated moral realizations occur but they seem always to be those that previously have been taught mechanically to the subject: in the cases of Americans they are those of Christianity, while orientals suddenly understand the inner meanings of Buddhistic doctrines.

Such a state could hardly be more contradictory to Objective Consciousness, as here defined. For in the latter instance surrounding objects, far from becoming "insensible," are perceived with a direct clarity never hitherto experienced, and there are no phenomena recognizable as "visions." Emotional realizations, moreover, are those of Objective Morality, which has only a slight relation to the versions of it taught to the Jews circa 30 A.D. or to East Indians at the time of Gautama the Buddha.

Bucke, of course, is but one among thousands of mystics but his views are more clearly expressed than those of most others. They may indicate the unnatural, because premature, experience of a state of consciousness beyond the achieved maturity of the subject; and they do demonstrate what happens in the subjective experience of the 'I'-entity, while still existing as I_O, when it is subjected to the conditions of the highest degree of consciousness directly from the Waking state.

But these experiences, although they are distorted instances of it, cannot fail to suggest something else: that there does exist some sort of conscious state beyond Awakeness, more expanded and objective than the latter and involving a more direct perception of the phenomena of the cosmos. The real potentiality of such a state must be shown by the very fact of its incorrect examples, just as the genuine possibility of paradic man is demonstrated by the existence of abnormal men.

The transformation of potentiality into actuality can be accomplished by the correct application of the correct techniques. And just as these exist for the transformation of the Waking state into one of Awakeness, so it is asserted that other such techniques can be employed—but only by one already sufficiently developed humanly to do so correctly—in order to attain to a state of Objective Consciousness from that of Awakeness.

The state of Objective Consciousness is described as follows. First, it includes a direct awareness of surrounding reality, the same type of active awareness, but directed upon different objects, that is involved in the awareness of the individual organism by "I" during periods of Awakeness. These surrounding objects are not imaginary or unheard-of; they are the ordinary objects of everyday life—inorganic and organic substances as we call them, living creatures, animals, men, planets and stars.

That all of these appear quite differently in different states of consciousness, cannot be doubted. We know that external reality presents itself otherwise to us in Waking than in Sleep and the briefest acquaintance with Awakeness will convince us that in this condition our perceptions of our surroundings again are very dissimilar to those of the Waking state. The common attribute of all these differences is plain: the greater the degree of consciousness, the greater the clarity with which the environment is perceived. That this clarity should once more be increased under the conditions of Objective Consciousness, is no more than expectable from our knowledge of the preceding conscious states.

Another accompaniment of Objective Consciousness is stated to be a novel clarity of emotional perception bringing one, among other consequences, to a full understanding of the precepts of Objective Morality. By this last term is meant the paradic emotional responses which a developed human being must manifest toward all external reality, not because he has been told to do so but because of his own inherent nature, such responses being manifested toward the objects of nature, his fellow-men and even the universe itself. By their own character emotional realizations of this kind cannot be other than objective, absolute and identical for all men. The innumerable subjective moralities of the Waking state are relative and vary with time and place but Objective Morality is absolute and unvarying for all genuine human beings at all times and all places.

There are five precepts of Objective Morality which can be only misrepresented verbally in the Waking state, and thus shall not be specified.* In any case to know them only verbally is to miscomprehend their essence almost completely. But to show the general nature of these precepts one of them will be stated.

*These injunctions have been stated publicly by others: Gurdjieff, G.I., *All and Everything*, First Series, Harcourt Brace & Co., New York, 1950, p. 386; Nott, C.S., *Teachings of Gurdjieff*, Routlege & Kegan Paul, London, 1961, pp. 206-8. The present writer does not intend to publish them for the curious who, in the Waking state, can only mislead themselves by memorizing them, nor does he think himself capable of formulating the last four of these principles correctly.

The first principle of Objective Morality is the obligation to maintain one's physical organism at its optimum state of health at all times. It is obvious that such a precept cannot vary from man to man, from locality to locality, from nation to nation, from race to race or from culture to culture. Like all the others it is, and must be, an absolute. But its real meaning can be appreciated only by one who has realized it for himself in the natural course of his own development, not when it exists merely as an external rule, imposed from outside.

For this reason the emotional responses accompanying Objective Consciousness cannot be stated profitably to those who have not as yet come to a personal realization of them during their own development. And this applies to all such emotional perceptions, not alone to those related to morality.

But with regard to the sensory perception of external reality we are curious to know at least under what guise this is supposed to be experienced in the fourth state of consciousness. Naturally we must recognize that to know such information verbally is not at all the same as understanding it fully from the realizations of one's own experience. Nonetheless, it would be satisfying to have some hint as to the aspect presented by the universe to one in the state of Objective Consciousness.

As just explained, we can have little confidence in the reports of the mystics who tell us of their experiences of Cosmic Consciousness; and in any case they speak much more of their emotional feelings than of external reality when their "minds become blank." Where, then, are we to look for reports in which we can place any confidence?

The findings of the Institute in this respect might be accepted by the reader with considerable reservation; and the writer has acknowledged already that he personally has nothing of this kind to offer. On all counts, therefore, it will be better to discover such formulations from those who have never heard of us and who could have had no interest in persuading us in any direction upon these matters. Fortunately there have been such people and we propose to turn to them in the present quandary.

One of the greatest civilizations known to us in the past or in the present is that of ancient Egypt. Its value-standards were objectively human in a sense that has never been exemplified so clearly since their time, for their whole culture was built around the concept of the fully developed human being as the goal toward which their government and their institutions were to be directed. Their art was oriented similarly and the design of their religion was the fulfillment of human potentiality. (11).

As to their art, for instance, it is stated that "Egyptian art was essentially aristocratic art. It was never concerned with art for its own sake or with the people as subject-matter for art. Egyptian art always expressed something beyond its own artistry. Ultimately it expressed a system of social values, an attitude towards life, a philosophy. Always the object of Egyptian art was the highest attainable manifestation of the type Man." (10). It was the same with all their other serious activities also.

Furthermore, the ancient Egyptians are not the figures of myth or legend. They actually existed and their later history has been recovered in much detail by the objective researches of reputable Egyptologists. Their realizations concerning the nature of the universe are likewise matters of record, not of traditional folklore à la anthropology.

As to the origin of these realizations, fortunately they are just of the sort for which we search here. They were said to be made from the state of consciousness which we are attempting to describe in the present chapter, and this was attained by means of some of the very techniques that we have been formulating in this book.

In this connection it will be well to point out that, according to competent authorities, the culture of ancient Egypt was predominantly a practical and hardheaded one (7) (9) and that the Egyptians themselves manifested no suggestion of mysticism, no credulity regarding ghosts or phantasms* and held the belief that the "soul" was a body every bit as physical as the organism with which they had been born. (6). The realizations to be mentioned were not vague, but concrete.

Their approach to these questions was not, as with us, through the techniques of Waking state science but, instead, it was through the psychological techniques which commence with the activation of consciousness. The latter was called by them Scrutiny or the method of the Eye of Hur. To begin with, Hur was Eye and only Eye, that is, he was pure observation. From this single activity only did there later develop all the attributes of Hur the Redeemer, based upon the altera-tion of the 'I'-entity from I_0 to "I", which is synonymous with the attainment of the state of Awakeness. The further disciplines of their religion were equally as practical as this first technique and were believed by them to lead eventually to the instatement in the qualified priest of a state of Objective Consciousness to which, however, they gave a religious rather than a scientific name.

Now these same techniques often have been employed by others under a somewhat different nomenclature, possibly by every genuine world-religion at the time of its original founding. We find a direct allusion to the method we have called the activation of consciousness, in the early Buddhistic writings (12); and everyone is familiar with the many references to our current "sleep" and the necessity for "awakening" from it, in the early Christian scripts. But these were religions that sought to supersede the Waking state and not by any means to condone it, considering it, to the contrary, to be the source of all our misfortunes or "sins".

For in the religions of the Waking state, regardless of their diverse

*For example, the acceptance of One Supreme God is not, in the writer's view, either credulous or superstitious. The totemistic opinions attributed to the Egyptians are assigned by those who quite plainly are themselves totemists of a slightly different variety; and the so-called "magics" of the later, degen-erated dynasties (and especially of Greek misinformants) obviously are not to be ascribed to the Egyptians earlier than Dynasty XIII.

origins, the communicant ignorantly accepts all sorts of false proposi-tions, i.e., he is the superstitious dupe of dogmas and creeds that for him are entirely unsupported assertions and indeed are often almost the opposites of the original formulations of his own faith. He is crassly biased in the most limited personal ways, i.e., he is the continual victim of the prejudices, the envies, the jealousies and the hatreds of his own subjectively watered-down religion. And he is prepared to, and always does, act upon his prejudiced misinformation, i.e., he is the proponent or the accomplice of persecutions and crusades against other religionists blindly following their somewhat different mechani-cal prejudices. "Faith" that is stupidity, "hope" that is illness and "love" that is a matter of no more than type and polarity, are the criteria of the Waking state religions which have devolved from their far superior prototypes.

But the ancient Egyptian religionist showed much more interest in discharging his obligation to God than in pretending a sancti-monious love of the Incomprehensible; and he manifested little confi-dence in being rescued by a mystical Grace, preferring to rely upon the more practical maxim that God helps him who helps himself. In the sober view of their competent contemporaries a great many Egyptians had helped themselves to such good effect that they had succeeded in achieving a humanly conscious state in which for the first time it became possible for them to assist the Deity in a manner properly owed to Him, rather than vice versa. This attitude not only manifests a correct human self-respect but in addition an objec-tive acquaintance with the realities of the universe.

With this brief and scarcely adequate introduction we may go on to inquire how the universe appeared to those who had completed successfully the techniques of a religion dedicated to the establish-ment of a genuinely human state of consciousness. We shall expect it to be a universe very different from the one we perceive in the Waking state.

The Waking state looks upon the universe as dying and in modern times has attempted to support this position by references to various scientific hypotheses. The moon is dead, the earth is dying, the sun itself gradually is losing its heat-energy and eventually will cool to the present temperature of the earth. The final upshot must be a dead-level state in which the smallest energy transfer becomes a self-contradiction and all differentiated forms of matter have been reduced to a homogenous uniformity. It may not be without significance that this democratic-socialistic view of nature has appeared precisely within those social systems which themselves have been undergoing a democratic-socialistic decline contemporaneously.

The view of Objective Consciousness, as formulated by the ancient Egyptian, was to the opposite effect. The derivation of the universe was from above to below, from the top to the bottom, from the complex to the simple. It began with the Universe-as-a-whole. Then from the Universe were derived the Galaxies, the various Milky Ways; within these, in turn, Suns and Solar Systems were differentiated. From Suns, Planets were derived; from Planets, their satellites or Moons. The direction of energy transformation, more and more diluted in the sense (as we should say) of progressively slower vibration-rates as the process continued, was from the Absolute to the satellites.

From this viewpoint the universe is, first of all, alive. Science anatomizes the corpse of the universe but Objective Consciousness contacts the living organism that is God's physical manifestation. The dead and dying cosmos of the Kant-LaPlace theory and of the second law of thermodynamics is seen from exactly the opposite direction. It is not only alive but growing, and the energy necessary for both maintenance and growth, coursing through it in every direction from its divine origin, is inexhaustible at its source.

But what was the further nature of this universe, as revealed to the Egyptians by those among them who were judged to be the greatest

in being? Contrary to popular misinformation, their view was mono-
theistic. They asserted "the existence of One Great God, self-produced,
self-existent, almighty and eternal, Who created the 'gods', the heav-
ens and the sun, moon and stars in them, the earth and everything
on it, including man and beast, bird, fish and reptile. They believed
that He maintained in being everything which He had created, and
that He was the support of the universe and the Lord of it all. Of
this God they never attempted to make any figure, form, likeness or
similitude, for they thought that no man could depict or describe
Him and that His attributes were quite beyond man's comprehension.
On the rare occasions in which He is mentioned in their writings, He
is always called 'Neter' (Nutsher,) i.e., God, and besides this He has
no name.... The management of the physical world and of the lives
and affairs of men was deputed by God to the 'gods,' 'goddesses' and
spirits." (5)

The aliveness of everything in the universe is a corollary of the
proposition that the universe is alive. And aliveness meant to the
ancient Egyptian just what it means to us, namely that its attributes
include consciousness, sentience, feeling and decision. There is no
distinction in this respect between the organic and the inorganic, and
the attribution of these qualities applies as directly to sticks and stones,
to substances and their material organization as it does to trees,
animals, men, planets. stars and solar systems.

Naturally an equal degree of these qualities was not attributed to
the innumerably different entities to be found in the universe. The
degrees vary from near-absence to a plenitude beyond our present
comprehension, but absolute absence is an impossibility for any actual
cosmic entity. Thus the degree of consciousness, sentience and so on
in a piece of lead is immeasurably less than in a human being, while
that of a star or of a solar system is immensely greater; but it is never
totally lacking. The ultimate criterion, as we should put it, is vibration-
rate; the lower the vibration-rate, the less the vivifyingness, and vice

versa. The paradic relationship of all these entities to each other is determined basically by their degrees of consciousness, which define their respective positions in the universe. Objective abnormality is evidenced by a departure from the manifestation of such correct relationships.

These propositions will permit us to comprehend, at least to some extent, the great difference in respect to such an entity as the sun, for example, when seen from the viewpoint of the Waking state as contrasted to that of Objective Consciousness.

The naive Waking view states that the sun is an orb composed of flaming gases, relatively stationary in space, about which the earth and other planets revolve; but on its own premises no such idea can be a rational one. We know very well that the sun is the center of powerful radiations throughout our solar system and that, when some of those radiations encounter the atmosphere of the earth, two of the resultant phenomena are those of light and heat. We also know that in the space between the sun and the earth there is a perceptible absence both of light and of heat, this space being dark and cold. The attribution of the light and heat directly to the sun itself is therefore as if we supposed there were a real little man inside the television set addressing us directly without the intermediation of any mechanism at all.

However, there are photographs to prove these gaseous assertions, it is said, photographs of the sun's rim taken during eclipses and showing huge flamelike protuberances shooting up from the surface. Most of us have seen such photographs but to take them literally is like arguing from a picture of the Kansas landscape that the earth is flat.

In the first place the photographs of the sun are taken through the earth's atmosphere, in which the solar radiations already have produced their effects, and their appearance, of light and heat. It is not remarkable that, seen through the atmosphere, they should resemble what in fact they cause there. In the second place, the camera sees only what the eye would see under the same conditions and what the eye sees in this case, is the illusion of the end-product. And in the third place the phenomena themselves are both indirect and complex; the correct interpretation of the physical nature of their source must likewise be indirect and complex, not the platitudinous observation of a big, bright, flaming sphere. That may be what it looks like through the medium of instrumentation—to direct observation in the Waking state it looks only like a very bright spot—but that is not at all what it is.

From the viewpoint of Objective Consciousness we are told that the sun, *imprimis,* is a creature possessing consciousness, sentience and decision. It is the center and organizer of other very large creatures, the planets, the source of their energies which it radiates to them and the director of their complicated courses. In the Egyptian religion the name of this creature is Re'. Of course the Egyptians also saw the protuberances (during eclipses) but they attributed these to illusions regarding the sun's disk (aton), and not to the real nature of the sun itself.

From the Egyptian view of cosmology it will be seen how the Egyptian priesthood understood the nature of so prominent a god as Re'. He was not supposed, in Greekish fashion, to be "the god of the sun," but instead he *was* the Sun, as we should put it with a capital S. For the instructed Egyptian our Sun-with-a-capital-S simply would be Re' deprived of his consciousness. In fact for the Egyptian there were not two terms, one for the sun and one for its god; the Sun was Re'.

This is a necessary consequence of the fact that the sun was taken as a being in its own right, a very different sort of being than a human one but nevertheless, like all the semi-independent parts of the universe, an entity possessing its own essential life, sentience and comparable psychic qualities. These qualities again were not the same as those of men but they were not on that account less vital or less psychic in their own degree and kind; rather, were they more so. The sun, then, was a creature and its attributes as a living being were at once very powerful and superior to the similar but lower attributes of such an entity as the moon.

What has been said of Re' will apply also and naturally to all the other entities of this cosmological character, and not only to them but likewise to all such smaller or larger creatures as may in similar fashion constitute semi-independent natural entities. Geb *is* the earth, not a god of the earth, and the cases of many others, such as Nut, Hapy and so on, are of the same kind. These make up the gods, solar and planetary, which are a part of Nutsher's physical manifestation.

But there is another class also of such gods, represented by Tehut, Ptah and like deities. They are not cosmological formations—suns, galaxies, planetary entities and so on; but they are what nowadays we would more customarily designate as cosmic forces. In this case the Waking state follows a much more complicated routine than does Objective Consciousness: first it identifies a series of phenomena as having certain characteristics in common; then it invents an abstraction drawn from their general behavior by which it seeks to offer an explanation of the phenomena, and it calls this abstraction a force; and finally it may personify such a force symbolically, even anthropomorphically, usually for purposes of art or religion. Conditioned toward such concepts by this long process, it is natural for the Waking state to see in gods like Tehut and Ptah "personifications" of the abilities of intellectual reason and of a "creative force" respectively.

But to the Egyptian observer there was no demand for such a lengthy course. To him the cosmos was alive and conscious and he was not in need of mental abstractions to assure him that both rational intellect and a living principle of pattern were cosmic attributes. Indeed they were more than attributes for him, since an attribute, too, is only an abstraction and these attributes of Nutsher, the One Great God, themselves became conscious creatures within His manifestation or universe, in relation to man. In other words, both the

intellect and the patterning characteristic of God were seen as objectified primarily and directly rather than indirectly and artificially
through the various steps first of abstraction and then of a rever-
sionary personification. God functioned in part by means of objective
reason and, in the universe that was His objective manifestation, His
reason itself became objectified as a great divine creature in the
service of God throughout His manifestation. Reason was Tehut, a
living and conscious god.

The case of Ptah is equally interesting and it is related also to the
many divine triads found in the Egyptian temples. In all phenomena
a third or patterning force is present which, in combination with the
positive and negative forces, permits the phenomenon to occur. Many
of the gods of Egypt existed in triads, one standing for the positive
force, one for the negative and one for the patterning, thus in
combination representing the wholeness of the divine activity under
consideration.

But these, of course, were of secondary derivation, the Great Triad
being that of God Himself, which necessarily is mirrored on smaller
scales throughout His manifested universe and its phenomena. But
if the phenomenon is objective, then so are the forces involved in it,
or, rather, these "forces" are merely analytical abstractions from the
objective entities actually taking part. Thus, although the Waking
state would call Ptah the personification of the third or patterning
force involved in all cosmic phenomena, for the Egyptian priesthood
Ptah was the objective divinity so engaged. In the universe Ptah was
God's Great Patterner, the sacredly conscious Designer. And many
more cases existed, analogous to those of Tehut and Ptah, for whose
discussion space is lacking. Together with the conscious cosmic formations they make up the category of cosmological gods.

This viewpoint also held that the fully developed human being
became both immortal and divine when he had attained to his full
maturity, including his attainment of Objective Consciousness and

Objective Reason. Such a man became a god also, although not of the cosmological kind. This type was named as Osir and a considerable number of the early kings, who by reason of their individual development had merited the position of heading the priesthood, were judged in all seriousness to have become such gods. Among them were Meny, Khenti, Djeser and numerous others.

Thus the living universe was peopled by three different classes of divine creatures: first, Nutsher, the One Supreme God; second, the cosmological gods, who were His sacred assistants and agents; finally, those human beings who had achieved divinity by their complete development and thus had become His assistants also, since they had succeeded in realizing their paradic place in the universe and had begun to discharge their fully human obligations, including those duties which they owed to the Creator, Nutsher Himself.

If these formulations, however foreign to our Waking state concepts, may be accepted as some of the consequences of Objective Consciousness, certain principles at variance with our customary ideas emerge at once.

The greater is not constructed from the lesser; to the contrary, the lesser is derived from the greater.

The universe did not manufacture God; God created the universe.

Parliaments do not make monarchs; the latter depute rights to parliaments.

Electorates do not bamboozle politicians; it is just the other way about.

A thunderstorm does not establish the weather; it is the former which is a result or symptom of the latter.

We call a baby human (although it doesn't look so) because its parents do look so.

And a human being belongs to the human species not because he has produced the human species but because it has produced him. In short, it is the type which evolves its instances, not the examples which fabricate the type. This is an argument that we have employed hitherto, namely, since the particular instance is always the example of a type, that from the occurrence of abnormal and undeveloped men we are entitled rationally to assume a paradigm from which they derive and which, by definition, establishes the paradic of manhood or humanity.

From the point of view of Objective Consciousness the fully matured and developed human being represents the genuine exemplification of the type, Man. But examples of this type may, and do, exist which do not, at this moment, represent its complete exemplification; so far they remain only approximations in various degrees of the type, Man. Six lesser derivations from the fully realized type exist. In order to avoid anything resembling esoteric nomenclature and to follow the terminology of the Gurdjieff Institute, let us label these simply as Man Seven, Six, Five, Four, Three, Two and One.

Man Seven, the complete exemplification of the type, is described as follows. He possesses Individuality (indivisible and unitary crystallization), Objective Consciousness and Objective Will. Since these correspond to the similar, though greater, attributes of the Creator Himself and since the man has made them his final and permanent possessions, in such a sense he may be said to be immortal in this universe.

Man Six is the same as Man Seven, with one exception. He has not as yet succeeded in making these attributes permanently and finally his own; and thus he can lose them.

Man Five has not as yet gained Objective Will but he has achieved an internal unity in which there is no conflict between or among his thoughts, his emotions and his deeds. He has thus attained to an objective Individuality in which his essential nature is indivisible and unified. He possesses a permanent conscious state of Awakeness and some experience of Objective Consciousness, which is the awareness, rather than the knowledge, of the true nature of reality, both internal and external. He is still in the unfortunate position, however, in which all he has gained, may be lost.

Man Four is in a transitional state that will be described further in a moment.

Man Three is automatic, mechanical and only passively conscious. He experiences no more than the Sleep and Waking states, the latter abnormal and the former usually so. Haphazard external events together with his hereditary constitution, of both of which he is the victim, cause all his reactions. And these latter are dominated by his head brain system mechanically, which controls and tyrannizes over the other two divisions of his nervous system. He is what we call an intellectualist.

Man Two is in the same condition as Man Three except that in his case external events determine his reactions chiefly through the second division of his nervous system, which automatically dominates the other two. He is an emotionalist.

Man One resembles Man Three and Man Two in all respects other than the dominating nervous system division. In his case it is the spinal cord division that controls his reactive behavior and thus he is of the practical personality type.

Man One, Two and Three are those whom we customarily encounter, since almost everyone is included among these types. Some, however, are combinations, and so they confuse us; but even these are always predominantly One, Two or Three and therefore fall within those categories. But it is said that the others exist and even that, under favorable circumstances, some contact may be made with them. Ordinarily this means that one may meet with a man one step higher in the scale than oneself, for it is unlikely that anyone more than one step removed could be recognized.

This brings us back to Man Four, who is an exception to the last statement. In the doubtful event of a meeting between Man Five and anyone of the types of One, Two or Three there exists the still more improbable possibility of any of the latter three profiting from it. In other words, mechanical man can learn from conscious man but only under two conditions: first, that he has become aware that he needs to learn and, second, that he greatly desires to learn. These two conditions are not set by Man Five but by the natures of Men One, Two and Three. That both of these conditions should happen to be met by any specific mechanically passive man at the time of the encounter, is highly improbable although not impossible.

There is then the added difficulty of recognizing Man Five accurately for what in fact he is, so that no charlatan shall be accepted as a substitute for the genuine article. In practice this means that in addition to his other predetermined attributes the candidate for instruction must possess a relatively unshakeable scepticism and that to the best of his ability he must test his instructor at the same time that his instructor is testing him.

Supposing all these requirements to have been satisfied, the mechanically passive man is only at the beginning of his efforts. Man Five can give him the necessary instructions and assistance, provided that the former may think them likely to be of some use, but only the candidate himself can provide the exertions demanded in order to overcome his own passivity and attain to a status more becoming as that of a human being.

To do so, it is not enough merely to hope and to wish; a definite technique must be employed and a definite discipline undergone. These again have neither been invented nor will they be enforced by the instructor, and only the candidate can hold himself to the difficulties of his task. Moreover, he is in the precarious position of a man who has loosed his hold upon one trapeze and has not as yet been able properly to grasp another. At any moment—through misunderstanding, through discouragement or laziness or many other misfortunes—he may lose all that so far he has acquired. He may even lose it permanently.

The position of Man Four is not an enviable one, it is a very dangerous one. It can be said only that the prize is great and that the chances taken must be commensurable. Through such means the candidate *may* become himself Man Five; if so, he will not be safe as yet but at least he will be on his way. And in any case Man Four constitutes the only secure pathway to the higher numbers, so that the choice is between attempting it or remaining forever what we are now.

We have now reviewed some of the ideas that are said to be associated with the state of Objective Consciousness. They are not the assertions of the writer for, as acknowledged, it is a conscious state which he has never experienced. They must, then, remain speculations, but speculation need not be entirely uncontrolled. It has been possible to discover others in whom some confidence may be placed since they have no axe to grind. Three items must characterize them: they must be unknown to us personally; they must repudiate all mystical revelations; there must be some reasonable basis upon which their assertions are alleged to rest. These are not easy qualifications to meet and so, if we have gone far into the past to find them, that can hardly be a reproach.

As to the state of Objective Consciousness itself, awareness is its criterion just as in the case of the other degrees of consciousness. But in this case it is asserted to be complete, the final degree of awareness possible for human beings.

In this connection it is necessary to distinguish between knowledge and awareness, and there is a large difference between them. We can know a great deal about the musculature of the human organism but such knowledge is always related primarily to abstractions and diagrams, disclosing general principles but never yielding an accurate description of the specific instance under consideration. The direct, active and non-identified awareness of some specific muscular equipment provides a quite different sort of information about it. At first it is far less detailed than the first kind, although eventually it may become even more so. Nor does it ever involve or depend upon generalities; it is precise and specific and applies directly to the organism observed, namely one's own.

This knowledge, of course, is not the kind deriving from Objective Consciousness but merely from the state of Awakeness. Knowledge derived from Objective Consciousness is of a similar sort, however; it arises from a direct awareness, not from a series of learned items. The difference is that its objects are not the details of an organism but the entities which make up the objective universe of reality. We have seen the considerable difference between these two contrasted ways of understanding the central body of our solar system, and the same will be characteristic of the ways in which all planetary and cosmic phenomena are apprehended respectively.

Objective Consciousness depends upon the presence of the proper energies required for its exercise and the subjective entity, as one of the factors in the triad making up a human being, possesses no energy sources within itself. Those sources all are possessed by a different factor of the triad, namely by the organism. It is only thence that the 'I'-entity, become objective, can call upon the energies demanded for its own conscious manifestation.

The energy sources for an organism through which Objective Consciousness may be manifested, are like those necessary for the manifestation of the state of Awakeness. Naturally they must be more potent and of course their active assimilation must be procured by the activity, specifically directed, of the 'I'-entity in question. They are not, however, mystical energies but once more purely physical and organic ones.

From the tables already given it will be seen easily where the required second conscious shock, necessary for the transformation of such energies organically, must occur. There exists an actual technique for this purpose, both anciently and modernly employed, but its description involves such terms as conscious labor and voluntary suffering, which are bound to be misunderstood in the Waking state. Furthermore, at present we have no accurate ordinary information regarding the physical nature of these specific energies as they are alleged to exist, so that no reasonable purpose can be served by discussing them at length. Here we seek only to show that theoretically they exist and that, if they exist actually, then they are no more mystical or fantastic than are the electricity and magnetism upon which we operate already.

To sum up the present chapter, we have been discussing a state of consciousness beyond that of Awakeness and attempting to discover what serious and rational allegations have been made about it. Its primary characteristic, as asserted, appears to consist in a direct awareness of phenomena external to the body, of both planetary and cosmic kinds, which provide a perception of physical and psychic reality much more clear and direct than that given in the state of Awakeness, and far beyond that of the Waking state. This view includes psychic as well as physical qualities but it appears also that these psychic qualities themselves are defined in purely physical terms, including those of mass, weight and vibration-rate.

More apposite to the subject of this book is the alleged condition of the 'I'-entity when related to external reality by the state of Objective Consciousness. The production of this conscious state is a result of the activity of the subjective entity itself but a series of activities more vigorous than those which lie behind Awakeness and for which further energy sources are required from the organism. Under these circumstances the 'I'-entity is no longer in the condition of I_O or even of "I"; it is now a genuinely human I, not only active but fully percipient and directive, and it represents the completely positive force in the triad of forces that composes the human being. In this situation the following relationships will obtain: positive factor—I;

negative factor—organism; relational or patterning factor—Objective Consciousness.

Assuredly much more could be said regarding the fourth state of consciousness, assertedly the highest attainable by man. But it would of necessity be more speculative than what has been discussed. The attempt has been only to make the potentiality of such a conscious state rationally intelligible and, if that has been accomplished, no more can be done under present conditions. For us it must occupy the status of a theorem, eventually perhaps to be established as an actuality but in the meantime neither to be accepted credulously nor to be repudiated incredulously.

The only sane attitude toward it must be one of correct scepticism. Many of the assertions of this chapter are certainly contrary to our Waking state opinions. Nonetheless they may be true.

REFERENCES IN THE TEXT OF CHAPTER VII.

1) Bucke, R. M. *Cosmic consciousness,* E. P. Dutton Co., N.Y., 1923.

2) Bucke, R. M. *Ibid.,* p. 23

3) Bucke, R. M. *Ibid.,* p. 268

4) Bucke, R. M. *Ibid.,* p. 283.

5) Budge, E.A.W. *Osiris and the Egyptian resurrection,* Warner, London, and Putnam, N.Y., 1911; pp. xxiii-xxiv.

6) Budge, E.A.W. *The book of the dead,* Warner, London and Putnam, N.Y., 1913; Introduction, Vol. I, pp 69ff., *passim.*

7) Budge, E.A.W. *Ibid.,* p. 121.

8) Eriksen, R. *Consciousness, life and the fourth dimension,* Alfred E. Knopf, Inc., N.Y., 1923; p. xii.

9) Gardiner, Sir A. *Egyptian grammar,* Oxford University Press, London, 1950; Introduction, 2nd Ed., p. 4.

10) Grey, Terence *Kings and queens of ancient Egypt* (Winifred Brunton *et. al.*), Hodder and Stoughton, London, 1926; Introduction, p. 9.

11) King, C. D. *Heritage, a social interpretation of the history of ancient Egypt,* Chapter I, The Religion of ancient Egypt; this book is as yet unpublished and no page references can be given.

12) Woodward, F. L. *Some sayings of the Buddha,* Oxford University Press, London, 1925; pp. 74-77.

chapter VIII

THE OUTCOME
OF THE INVESTIGATION

LET US TAKE STOCK of the situation and see what has been determined by the inquiry. We began our analysis of the consciousness problem with a discussion of the three long-standing and contrasted views regarding the nature of consciousness—those of the subjectivist, the objectivist and the parallelist schools of thought. Let us ask if these conflicts can be reconciled as a result of what we have found.

It is uncertain just how the subjectivist considers the term, consciousness, but it would seem that he supposes it to be some sort of primary entity which in a rather mysterious manner creates or in some way determines the structures through which it is mediated. The organism itself, in fact, would appear to be viewed as a reflection of the consciousness that is prior to it and more fundamental than it.

The objectivist, on the other hand, thinks of consciousness as a result or as a by-product of its mediators, usually of the nervous system operations which he believes to cause its occurrence. Sometimes he identifies consciousness with psychonic energy, sometimes with other entities characteristic of the organism, but always it is a *thing,* an objective item ultimately analyzable in the terms of physics.

The parallelist just abandons the puzzle, setting the organism and its neurology to one side and consciousness to the other, while maintaining that the two derive from different worlds of discourse and that their terms must be incommensurable, although the events to which they refer respectively, may run parallel to each other.

We have seen, however, that consciousness is not an entity, as the subjectivist often views it, and that even less is it the kind of concrete thing to which the objectivist frequently commits himself. Consciousness is a relationship; and a relationship is neither an entity nor a thing, it is a state of connection between two different entities or things. A relationship can exist only as a reference which two other items bear to each other. In the case of human consciousness this reference is that which the subjective entity bears to the human organism or vice versa. The labels by which we denote the different states of consciousness, fundamentally describe this relationship in general terms.

But if one accepts that consciousness is a particular relationship between the subjective entity and the objective organism, one has already assigned subjectivism to one item of the two and objectivism to the other, so that neither term remains proper for the relationship subsisting between them.

If a specific relationship between protons and electrons constitutes an atom, then neither the protons nor the electrons can be designated as atomic. It is the electromagnetic field of the atom that patterns the constituent entities into their result, the atom, because the atom is the phenomenon which appears as a result of the proton-electron relationship. And in the same way it is the state of consciousness which establishes the particular relationship between subjective entity and objective organism that defines the specific condition resulting, e.g., Sleep, Waking and so on. It is evident, therefore, that one can be a subjectivist in reference to the 'I'-entity or an objectivist in reference to the organism but that one can be neither when the matter under consideration is consciousness or the relation between the foregoing separate items.

As to parallelism, it simply begs the question, and that is an attitude which cannot be adopted successfully, either.

The difficulty in this problem arises from the failure to distinguish accurately between the three independent but mutually interacting factors that are the real components of the problem, namely the 'I'-entity, the organism and the third factor of consciousness which relates them to each other. Once the distinction has been made, we can see that subjectivism is appropriate to one factor and objectivism to another but that neither the subjectivist nor the objectivist view can be appropriate to the third factor called consciousness. The understanding of the true situation depends upon a clear apprehension that three factors are involved and that the third one, consciousness, corresponds to the field factor in physics and biology and cannot be designated by the terms respectively relevant to the other two.

The reconcilation of the subjectivist and objectivist views can be accomplished only by pointing out that the first is correct in reference to one factor of the whole human integer and the second correct in reference to another but that what relates these two factors to each other is an additional field factor whose actual function is reconciling and which therefore cannot be described in terms of the items whose mutual relationship it establishes.

In continuing the discussion it will be well to refer again to the four basic states of consciousness and to the distinction that must be made between these states *per se* and the different levels which exist within each of them respectively.

Thus there are different *stages* within the Sleep state. They have been identified by Blake and Gerard, *op. cit.*, as 1) light sleep, 2) deep sleep and 3) very light end-sleep. Within stage 1) Davis, Davis, Loomis, Harvey and Hobart, *op. cit.*, have distinguished no less than three separate levels: B) a progressive drowsiness as the subject falls asleep; C) a definite light sleep; D) a deeper sleep. Their stage E) corresponds to the deep sleep level of Blake and Gerard's stage 2), above.

During the progress of Sleep these levels do not follow any constant course. The levels change upwards towards Waking and downwards towards deep Sleep, probably due chiefly to the altering dream content as the subject automatically expends the unbalanced energies remaining in the body at the conclusion of the previous Waking state. Besides these more or less legitimate Sleep levels, there are various pseudo-Sleep conditions such as narcosis, anaesthesia and so on, externally forced upon the organism through the administration of drugs, poisons and the like.

Within the Waking state we may distinguish at least two typical stages, the Waking stage proper, itself of quite light hypnosis, and the stage of genuine hypnotic trance wherein the typical suggestibility of the Waking state is highly exaggerated. Within the first of these stages we find various levels of greater and lesser daydream, sometimes lapsing into pure phantasy. In addition, there are the generally conceded pathological conditions of neurosis and psychosis, which occupy their own levels of the Waking state.

When we come to the state of Awakness, different degrees of it can be differentiated, although there are probably insufficient data for formal identication at different levels. The writer's first experiences of this state, detailed previously, are a case in point. The state of Awakeness is defined by the subject's accurate current awareness of his own organic phenomena. In the instances cited it will be recalled that his attention was caught by quite novel perceptions of the immediate external environment, with the result that the very efforts, correctly directed, which had produced the new type of perception, were automatically abandoned and that the conscious state itself then disappeared almost immediately. The external perceptions were not in themselves abnormal but the point is that they are only by-products of the state of Awakeness. When one permits one's attention to be captured by them, the basis of the state itself—which basis is organic awareness—is destroyed, whereupon its by-products vanish in quick succession.

To maintain the state of Awakeness for any appreciable length of time costs great effort and is exceedingly difficult for the beginner, but its definition is correct and the state must disappear at once when *for any reason* those efforts cease. Undoubtedly further differentiations could be made within the general state of Awakeness but we are not in a position accurately to do so at present.

Very probably there are also different levels to be distinguished within the state of Objective Consciousness but, here again, it is impossible to speak with proper accuracy. One conjectures that this state must comprise within its general boundaries lesser and greater degrees of perceptual clarity, depending upon the varying utilization of the demanded energies by the 'I'-entity involved. But when there is so little reliable knowledge of this state of consciousness, it seems bootless to discuss mere conjecture.

The conclusions we can draw concerning the relations of the 'I'-entity within the four primary states of consciousness will be more valuable. Over the span of these different states the 'I'-entity itself undergoes a progressive development or, to put it somewhat better, it is the progressive development of the 'I'-entity from the condition of I_0 to that of I which determines and instates the successively possible states of consciousness. This development depends upon the utilization of organic energies not usually employed and some of which can be made available only by an unaccustomed activity of the 'I'-entity, correctly directed and made possible by a small initial amount of such energy already present under ordinary circumstances.

During this process we have the 'I'-entity altering its own state from the original condition of mere necessary postulation to a degree of real objectivity as the Awakeness state is established and, finally, to complete objectivity when the final state of Objective Consciousness is permanently confirmed. In the two latter conditions the 'I'-entity has changed its own status from that of a required concept to that of an objective entity in its own right, a change which it is almost impossible to formulate adequately in the verbal symbols employed in the Waking State. However, it is quite possible to tabulate the successive relations among the three factors that constitute a human being under these different conditions:

Patterning Factor or Conscious State	Positive Factor or Active Component	Negative Factor or Passive Component
Sleep	Spinal Cord System	Head Brain and Basal Gangliar Systems
Waking	Total Organism	I_0
Awakeness	"I"	Total Organism
Objective Consciousness	I	Organism and Environment

Table 3: Conscious States and Factors

Taking the first or Sleep state, we find here that the subjective entity is absent when the condition is a paradic one. What this means, is that, when the Sleep state is manifested correctly, the 'I'-entity is unconscious, that is, it is absent temporarily from the relationship constituting the wholeness of the human integer. This does not signify that it has vanished from the realm of reality. It shows only that, for the time being, the subjective entity has become totally inert and in such a condition manifestly it cannot continue at this time the relationship to the organism which determines a conscious state in reference to the latter. That is a result of the circumstance that ordinarily the 'I'-entity is only a concept, a concept which is absent from experience in deep and genuine Sleep.

When we consider the usual abnormal type of Sleep, full of dreams and conflicts, we encounter all kinds of delusional interpretations of the fact. We do not refer here to the hallucinatory content of the dreams themselves but to the later meanings assigned to the phenomena. These vary from the sexually overweighted interpretations of psychoanalysis to such strange notions as that the 'I'-entity in Sleep is touring about the world or even the universe, or that it is revisiting the scenes of "previous lives," as if it were possible for "reincarnations" to take place before the prior accomplishment of incarnation itself. This last idea is born of the inability to recognize the significance of the simple prefix, "re-." Anyone who supposes that he has accomplished the tremendous task of incarnation in the Waking state plainly is committing an egregious error; it was one of the subtlest "mysteries" of the early Christian doctrine and is the final goal of the complete state of Awakeness.

All these delusions occur, not in the Sleep state but in its successor condition, that of Waking. They are typical rationalizations, set up to offer some explanation of the preceding dream experiences. But the dream experiences arise in fact from the random discharge of cerebral nervous energy upon the final arrival platforms of the sensory centers in the head brain system during its relative insulation from the spinal cord division of the nervous system. They are not evidences of journeys in space and time; and their attempted subjective explanations are only, as has been said, delusional interpretations of what seem to the subject to be more or less chaotic experiences undergone during Sleep.

During the Waking state the subjective entity exists in the condition of I_0, that is, of a conceptual postulation whose only function is a passively experiential registration of what is occurring willy-nilly in the organism with which it is associated. This condition, in which all of us spend most of our time, is thoroughly abnormal and its abnormality consists primarily in the passive role played by the 'I'-

entity in that state. The resulting relation between the organism and I_O is one in which the former manifests actively, the latter passively. The derived relationship is the Waking state of consciousness, confused, often blurred and frequently hazy with daydream. One of the worst features of this state is that the subject, never having experienced anything better, is quite unaware not only of his organism but of the predicament that his subjective experience is unrepresentative even of the verbalisms upon which he relies vaguely. All this is a consequence of his own passivity, which he suspects still less when it is at its peak.

In the state of Awakeness these misfortunes are obviated, simply because the relationship has been changed; the 'I'-entity in this condition becomes active with respect to the organism, which now takes up its correctly passive part in the total manifestation. The upshot is a great increase in clarity of experience, the ability to make far sharper distinctions than formerly, and a feeling of active well-being scarcely ever achieved in the foregoing Waking state.

As to Objective Consciousness it can be said only that the above mentioned attributes are allegedly carried over to the perception of the total environment, not simply focussed upon the organism with a by-product of perceptual clarity in reference to the *immediately* surrounding environment. Other attributes of this state have been denoted previously to the best of our ability and nothing is to be gained by repeating them here.

The key to all these alterations is subjective activity, activity involves effort, and effort is disagreable to all of us. Moreover, this particular subjective effort is much more strenuous than the most vigorous which we ever have been forced to make under external compulsion, and in this case the compulsion, in addition, must come from inside. The cause of this apparently paradoxical situation is that at present the organic energies demanded for such efforts are almost entirely lacking to us and that, as a condition of their acquirement,

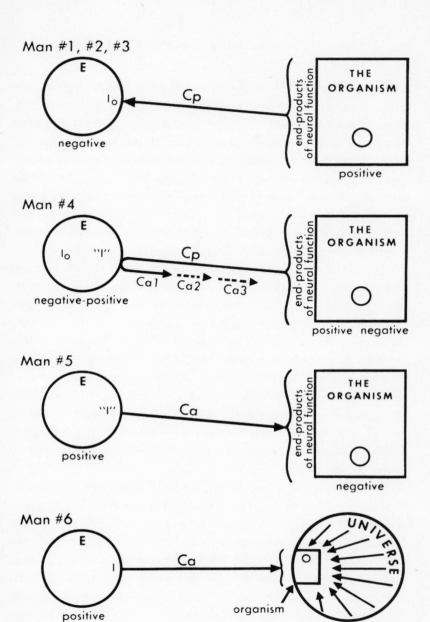

Man #1, #2, #3

E
I_o
negative

C_p

end-products of neural function

THE ORGANISM

positive

Man #4

E
I_o "I"
negative-positive

C_p
C_{a1} C_{a2} C_{a3}

end-products of neural function

THE ORGANISM

positive   negative

Man #5

E
"I"
positive

C_a

end-products of neural function

THE ORGANISM

negative

Man #6

E
I
positive

C_a

organism

UNIVERSE
O

negative

I_o = postulated 'I'—entity
I_o-"I" = transitional 'I'—entity
"I" = pseudo — 'I'—entity
I = genuinely human 'I'—entity

C_p = passive Consciousness
C_{a1}, C_{a2}, C_{a3} =
    transitional consciousness
C_a = active Consciousness

DIAGRAM VI

the preliminary efforts must be made with what meager supplies may at first be available. When the proper energies have been acquired, these earliest exertions will seem relatively negligible but at that time, also, proportionally greater efforts will be necessary if what has just been achieved, is not again to be lost. But activity and effort are the touchstones of the human being as such and the extent of our humanity perhaps can be judged by our individually voluntary assent to this proposition.

Nevertheless, in our present situation willingness, however eager, is not sufficient. There must be knowledge, there must be accurate instruction, there must be available a rigorously defined discipline in which one may take part together with others and, above all, there must be the leadership of a *competent* guide.

A small sample of such disciplines has been indicated in Chapter II, in order to give the reader some idea of their nature, but it is necessary to repeat that even so little as that is of the utmost danger if undertaken on one's own initiative in the absence of the most competent supervision. The danger is that, due to slight but unavoidable errors, one may become thereby a real freak and lose one's genuine human potentiality forever. Again it is emphasized that such techniques *must not* be embarked upon alone, for they *cannot* so be employed successfully.

In considering this whole subject, the author has sought to acknowledge his great debt to the original Gurdjieff Institute and to the propositions that it formulated a considerable number of years ago. Not only the propositions but the practical techniques then employed have the most direct bearing upon the problem of the nature of human consciousness. It has been the attempt here to analyze and otherwise to examine these propositions from the scientific viewpoint. That in our present state no such investigation can be complete, appears conclusive. But the genuine scientific outlook is nonetheless an impartial one and a scientific elucidation of some of the Institute propositions does, in the writer's opinion, add to the clarity of their formulation. It has been hoped, incidentally, thus to make them more accessible to the analytical mentality to which many of us find ourselves preconditioned.

The supply of the demanded energies for the states of Awakeness and of Objective Consciousness is a physical matter. The activation of consciousness will afford an increase of our ordinary organic energies in a purely physical way. But such activation nevertheless remains dependent upon a psychologically positive action that in itself cannot originate from what we now call physical causes, not, that is, from the organism but only from the subjective factor that is associated with it. For this reason it is necessary to acknowledge the balance of subjectivity-objectivity, not only in the natural development of the human being but similarly in his constitution as a genuine human integer.

This synthesis relates pointedly to the nature of human consciousness. Since consciousness is the relation between organic phenomena and the subjective entity which experiences them, the states of consciousness represent basically the different degrees of clarity referring to that relationship.

In Sleep it is obscured and indefinite; in Waking it is more detailed but directed externally and, because internally passive, cloudy and filled with daydream, delusion and semi-trance. In Awakeness the relationship is far clearer, representing a direct awareness of the organic phenomena of the associated body and thus of the instrument through which all perceptions of the external world are mediated. When the instrument itself is activated indirectly in this way, the perceptions it mediates, in turn must become clearer, as an early by-product of the conscious activity. In Objective Consciousness, so it is said, this clarity is carried over to the entire external world, resulting in a direct awareness of the true reality of the universe in which we live. This last statement may or may not be correct but it is, at the least, a rational and common sense extrapolation of what we do know about the first three states of consciousness.

The objection to these ideas is that they are not immediately apparent in our ordinary experience, including our laboratory experience. And of course they are not. The change to which this discussion points, is primarily a change of conscious state; and the result of *that* change must be an alteration of experience to include items and implications lacking in the Waking condition. So long as our consciousness remains of the Waking variety, some, though not all, of these propositions cannot be confirmed. But if the intensified degree of consciousness that we designate as Awakeness, be attained, then these propositions become confirmable through the very same processes and steps that constitute the present scientific method.

It is difficult to make clear that this condition of proof is an alteration of consciousness, not of the items of reality that are confirmable in varying degree in different states of consciousness. Such real items remain constant always; but their perception can become both clearer and more comprehensive if the viewpoint (or consciousness) from which they are perceived, is altered. That is the change which makes possible the perception of physical phenomena and the relations between them which, under other circumstances, remain either obscure or undetectable.

That this reasoned background for judging the various conditions of the 'I'-entity is not a mere phatasmagoria of subjective speculation, is demonstrated, in the writer's opinion, by the circumstance that practical psychological techniques exist — and have existed for thousands of years — whereby the alteration of the 'I'-entity from passivity to activity can be brought about. Of his own knowledge he is aware that such techniques in fact do accomplish their purpose, at least insofar as concerns the inauguration of the change from I_0 to "I". It is true that he can offer no personal evidence beyond that point but, since the first change (or any change at all) is by far the most crucial of the whole series, it would seem that the fundamental point at issue is established and that the further developments to be expected from the continued prosecution of such techniques may be taken, at least provisionally, as rational assumptions.

So much for the practical aspects of the matter. As for the intellectual, the case appears to be both logical and reasonable. Regarding its emotional posture, there cannot be the same assurance. Propositions such as these frequently arouse a tremendous enthusiasm, which often gives the appearance of being both false and fanatical. During these enthusiasms all perspective seems to be lost and their victims soon acquiesce in the most preposterous credulities. For these it is difficult to find a legitimate excuse and such emotional responses would appear to be definitely abnormal. It is also true that, although often occuring, they are not a necessary consequence in all cases, perhaps not even in most cases.

Finally it is necessary to reflect that the states of consciousness which we have labelled as Awakeness and as Objective Consciousness, are not asserted to be actualities for us, but only potentialities. Regarding potentialities, there are two kinds, the real and the unreal. An example of the former is reaching between one's legs and picking up some object from the ground; of the latter, reaching between one's legs and touching the back of one's neck with the palm of the hand.

In the writer's opinion there is reason to accept that the two potential states of consciousness discussed are of the real variety. The final conclusion is that all the four states of consciousness do exist in fact, either as real actualities, or conditionally, as real potentialities for creatures of the human kind. Through them and their attainment the differing degrees-of-being of human beings are to be defined objectively.

index

bnormalities of Sleep, 47-48
  effects on organism, 47-48
bnormality of Waking state, symptoms, 82
C brain wave measurements, 78
C brain waves, characteristic in Waking State, 81
C electrical measurements, 46, 78, 99
C electroencephalograms, 5
  as measurement of sleeping states, 5
C properties of organs, 83
ctivation of consciousness, 27-43
  steps in, 34-41
ctive awareness, effect of, 36
  effect on cerebellar lobes, 116
  how manifested, 35-43
  as third step of anabolic process, 115
ctive vs. passive registration in food anabolism, 105
fferent block, 67, 69, 70, 77
fferent input in Sleep, 66
lterations of perception in Awakeness, 119-127
nabolic processes, 72, 74-79
nabolic transformations, 82-97
nabolism, 74, 82, 102, 104-105, 108, 109, 113, 115, 118
  octave of, 75-86, 102, 108-109
  steps of, 84
naesthesia, 53-54
  as opposed to true Sleep, 53
nalysis, necessary absence of in awareness techniques, 36
rrival platforms of nervous systems, 17-18
  function of in sensation and imagery, 67-68
  in Sleep, 47
tom, constitution of, 156
wakeness, 99-129, 158-167
  advantage of, 121-128
  characteristics of, 49-50, 100-102, 119-128
  comparability of experiences, 126-127
  difficulties in describing, 119-120
  duration of, 120-127
  in early Christian texts, 138
  experiences of, 119, 121-128
  obstacles in assembling data, 99-100
  predictability of achieving, 126-127
Awareness, as catalyst, 116
  compared to action of light, 116
  state beyond, 134
  of gross physical behavior, in Waking State, 91-92
  through sensations, 33

Babinski reflex, 57, 66, 77
Basal ganglia, 17-18
Basal gangliar response, 24
Basal gangliar system, 17-19, 69-71, 90-91, 92, 112, 160
  during Sleep, 69-71
Basal gangliar and autonomic system, in Waking state, 86
Behavior, present sequence of, 26
  reversal of sequence of, 26-27
  sequences of in active consciousness, 26-43
Behaviorism, 3
Behavior sequences of Waking state, 88
  abnormality of succession of parts in, 89
Blockages of nervous system during Sleep, 66-67
Blood, during Sleep, 56
  as reinforcement in anabolic processes, 76
Body temperature during Sleep, 55
Book of the Dead, 41
Brain and neural patterns, during Sleep, 57, 59
Brain waves, in Sleep, 58-59
Brodmann's Area, 17, 24, 67
Bucke, 3, 133-134
Buddhistic writings, 138
Burr, Harold Saxton, 4-5
  work of, 83

Carbon dioxide, in relation to Sleep, 57, 60
Cardiac energy, 84, 109-110, 111
Catalepsy, not related to Sleep, 65
Catalysis, compared with third step in energy transformation, 115-116
Cataplexy, not related to Sleep, 65
Cerebellar cortex, characteristics of, 112-118

Cerebellar lobes, 107, 114, 116
 functions of, 116-117
Cerebellum, 17-19, 106-108, 111, 117, 118
 effects of removal of, 107
 energy to, 108
 function of, 106-109
 input and output of energy to, 112-118
 as integrator of human organism, 117-118
 neural output to, 112
 nonfunctional aspect, 107-109, 113-118
 "silent" areas, 112
Cerebral arrival platforms, 106
Cerebral cortex, 112, 113, 114-118
 related to Sleep, 62, 63, 65
Cerebral output, 107
Cerebral system, in Waking state, 86
Cerebrum, 57, 86, 106-107, 108
 in anabolic transformation, 85
 as correlation center, 114
 part in energy transformation, 106
Cheyne-Stokes breathing, in Sleep, 57
Christenson theory of Sleep, 61
Christian scripts, "awakening" in early texts, 138
Circulatory system, during Sleep, 56
Clairvoyance, credibility of, 132
Claparède's "instinct" theory of Sleep, 62
Clarity, degrees in four states of consciousness, 165-167
Compassion, in Awakeness, 123-124
Consciousness, activation of, 29-43
 as active patterning factor, 96
 attributes of passivity, 22-27
 in Buddhistic writings, 138
 as by-product of neural or other phenomena, 12
 as co-existing psychological and physiological phenomena (parallelism), 12
 definitions of, 11
 as degrees of clarity, 165-167
 difference from thought process, 32
 as electrochemical energy, 4
 as field factor, 157
 field theory of, 13-15
 objectivist definition, 3-4
 objectivist view, 4, 155
 parallelist view, 155-156
 potentially active, 21

as primary reality, 11-12
 problem of, 11-27
 as relationship, 156
 resultant phenomena, 4
 scientific analysis of, 11-29
 states of, 45-51
 states of according to Bucke, 133
 subjectivist view, 155
 theories of, 11-15
 in Watson's view, 3
Control of behavior in Waking state, 91
Correlation centers. See Cerebellum, Cerebrum, Cortex.
Cortex, 17-19, 68, 91
 correlations centers of, 18, 68-69, 91 115
 frontal lobes, 18, 30
 function in Sleep and consciousness 67-69
 "silent" areas of, 66
Cortical inhibition in Sleep, 62
Cortical integrations, 92
Cortico-ponto-cerebellar tract, 108, 11 113, 114
 energy lost at, 108-109
Cosmic Consciousness, attributes of, 13 133
 as distinct from Objective Consciou ness, 45
 features of, 50
Cosmic forces, 144
Cosmology, Egyptian view of, 143-145
Criticism, necessary absence of in awar ness techniques, 35
Curve of sleepiness, 61

Dangers of techniques of active awar ness, 42, 164
DC electrical measurements, 46, 78, 99
DC field alterations, 59, 81
DC field measurements, 78
DC field of human body, 5
 relation to sleep, 5
DC tracings in Waking state, 81
Delusions of activeness in Waking stat 89-97
Democratic-socialistic view of nature, 14
Devils, attitude of Gurdjieff toward, 6
Digestion, during Sleep, 55
 stages of, 73, 82
Digestive processes, 74-80, 102-106
 to acquire energy, 74-80

beyond gaseous state, 84
Dream deprivation, effects of, 78
Dream imagery, 68-69
Dream phenomena, effect on afferent
    impulses, 67
Dreams, 47
    effects of on organism, 47
    as result of unexpended energies, 49
Dubois theory of Sleep, 60
Duval and Cajal theory of Sleep, 62

E.E.G. data, during Sleep, 58
Efferent arc as affected by synergy, 107
Efferent blocks, in Sleep, 66, 67, 69, 77
Egypt, ancient culture of, 41, 137-138
    art, goal of, 137
    concept of human being in, 137, 145-
        146
    gods of, 141, 144-145
    mysticism in ancient, 137-138
    religion of, 2, 137
    techniques of awareness in, 41
    value standards, 137
    view of divine kings, 146
Electrical AC properties, 83
Electrical energy of human organism, 73-
    74
    blocks in, 102, 103, 104-105
Electrical energy-production, 102-106
Electrical nerve impulse propagations,
    106
Electrical potential differences, 104
Electrical stage of anabolism, production
    of, 85
Electrical system in living organism, 83
Electrocardiograph, 83
Electroencephalograph, 83
Electromagnetic fields, 71, 103-104
Electromagnetic properties, of proto-
    plasm, 83
Emotion, 4
    in Waking state, 90-91
Emotional energies, 73
Emotional experience, 16-18
Emotional man, as abnormal state, 86-87
End-products of neural function, 19
Energies, expended unequally in Waking
    state, 49
    types of, 84
    use of in Waking state, 86-97
Energy-input as third form of organic
    food, 105
Energy reinforcement, active awareness

as third shock, 114-115
Energy sources, 74-77, 82-85, 102-109,
    111-114
    food (chemical), 74-77, 109
    gaseous (nasal), 75-77, 82, 83-85, 102,
        105, 108-109, 111
    neural, 109, 110, 114
    use of, 102-106
Energy transformation, path of, 106-116
Environment, impression of in Awake-
    ness, 123-125
    as originator of action in Waking
        state, 90
    perception in four states of awareness,
        160-167
Ericksen, 3, 132
Esotericism, 6
Experience, categories of, 16-18
    raw material of sensory, emotional
        and mental, 16-18
Experiencer as distinct from experience,
    13-14
Experiential abnormality of Waking state,
    86
Experiential function, reversal of in Wak-
    ing state, 89
Experiment, technique of, 127
External reality, in Awakeness, 120
External reinforcement, for energy trans-
    formation. See Shock.
Extraction in digestive processes, 84
Eye of Hur, as technique of Conscious-
    ness, 41.
    See also Scrutiny.

Food, forms of, 75, 76-77, 82-85, 102, 105,
    108, 109, 114
    "impressions", 105
    nasal, 75-79, 82, 84, 102, 105, 108,
        109, 111
    neural, 109, 110, 114
    oral, 77, 82, 83-85, 102, 105, 108-109
Food intake, effect of on consciousness,
    72-78
Fourth Way, 94
Free will, as delusion, 89-90
"Functional" block, in Sleep, 66

Geb, 144
Genetic energies, 84-85, 109-110, 111
Glands during Sleep, 56
Gnostics, 41

God, concept of in ancient Egypt, 138,
     139, 141-145
  as monotheism, 138
Gurdjieff, Georges Ivanovitch, 5-6, 94,
     100-101
Gurdjieff Foundation in New York, 7
Gurdjieff Institute, 94, 100, 101, 118. *See
     also* Institute for the Harmonious
     Development of Man.
Gurdjieff method of instruction, 6

Hallucinations, as compared with Awake-
     ness, 124
Hapy, 144
Hart, Bernard, 2
Head brain system, 160
  during Sleep, 69-71
Health, as first principle of Objective
     Morality, 136
Heart action during Sleep, 56
Hess theory of Sleep, 61
Hibernation, as opposed to true Sleep, 53-
     54
History of Crime, 97
Human being, in ancient Egyptian view,
     145-146
  aspect of when seen in Awakeness,
     123, 125
  characteristics of fully conscious, 147
  definition of, 20
  as distinct from human organism, 20
  pattern of transition from passive to
     active, 147-151
  as seen by Objective Consciousness,
     147-150
  types of, 147-150
  as "victim of circumstances", 88-89
Human organism, in balance, 117-118
  basic components, 103
  definition of harmonious, 87
  factors of, 71
  magnetic and electrical properties, 83
  as mechanism for transformation of
     electrical energy, 73
Human thought as physical mass, 6
Humoral theories, objections to, 61
  of Sleep, 60-61
Hur the Redeemer, in Egyptian religion,
     138
Huxley, Aldous, 14
Hypnosis, compared to Waking state, 34,
     48, 132

Hypnotic state, in Waking, 48
Hypophysis, effect of extirpation of o
     Sleep, 61
Hypothalamus, in control of consciou
     ness, 64-65

"I" as distinct from "It", 15, 38
"I" as entity, 15
Identification with one's physical orgar
     ism, 37
  separation from, 37-41
"I"-entity, as active thing, 127-128
  in Awakeness, 162
  as core of subjectivity, 14-15
  initiation of behavior of, 26
  as I_O, in Sleep, 78-79
  as objective, 127-128
  in Objective Consciousness, 162
  related to external reality in Objectiv
     Consciousness, 152-153
  relations within four primary states o
     consciousness, 159-167
  in Sleep, 160-161
  in state of Io, impressions received ir
     106
  in Waking state, 94-95, 161
"I"-entity activity, 25-27
  from Waking to Awakeness, 72
Imagery, phenomenon of, 67-68
Impressions, as energy manifestation
     106
  processes of, 67-69
  neurological history of, 106-116
  as third form of natural food, 105
Institute for the Harmonious Develop
     ment of Man, 1, 5, 7, 38, 41, 8
     94, 100-101, 118, 126-127, 13
     164
  findings of in relation to Objectiv
     Consciousness, 136
  terminology for types of human being
     147-151
Integration of objectivism and subjectiv
     ism, 7-8
Intellectual man, as abnormal state, 86-8
Introspection, in Waking state, 92
Intuition, credibility of, 132
"I_O", as entity, 15
  condition of "I"-entity, defining char
     acteristics, 37
  interpretations of reality by, 24
  metamorphosis to "I", 128

passivity of, 20-27
as subjective entity, 20
in Waking state, 95

ant-LaPlace theory of universe, 140
atabolism, 74-75
empf, Edward J., 3
ings, in ancient Egypt, 146
leitman's theories of Sleep, 60, 61, 65
nowledge, as different from awareness,
    150

evels of Sleep, 69-71, 157-158
ight-Gaining, technique of, 41
iver, function of in anabolism, 75-76, 82,
    112
iving cells, magnetic poles, 83
    magnetism of, 104
oci of anabolic transformations, 85

Iagnetic and electrical states of matter,
    83-84
Iagnetic disruption of brain systems as
    cause and definition of Sleep, 71
Iagnetic fields, 104
Iagnetic stage of anabolism, production
    of, 85
Iarston, William, 3
Iediations, use of in active awareness, 39
Iemory, definition of, 32
Iental energies, 73
Iental experience, 16-19
Iental processes, effect of on awareness,
    36-43
Ionkey, visual discrimination of, 93
Ionotheism, in Egyptian religion, 138-
    139, 140-141
Iultiple personalities, 94-95
Iystical experiences, 5, 40
    as distinct from active consciousness,
    40

Iarcosis as opposed to true Sleep, 53-54
Iasal food, 76-77, 82, 83-85, 102, 105,
    108-109, 111
Ierve impulse conduction, 83
Ierve impulses, during Sleep, 69-71
    during Waking, 68
Ierve tracts, 17
Iervous system, effects of defect on con-
    sciousness, 19-20

neurological divisions of, 16-18
    in Sleep, 55-60
Neter, 141
Neural electrical energy, 115
Neural food, 109, 110, 114
Neural functioning, deficiencies of, 20
Neural theories of Sleep, 60, 61-66
Neurological event, non-active interpreta-
    tion of, 24
    and sensation, 4-5
Neurological phenomena, 2-3
Non-identification with organism, 37-43
Normal, definition of, 46
    term misused, 46
North and south poles of living cells, 83,
    104
Nutsher, 144-146. See also Neter.

Objective Consciousness, 51, 131-167
    abnormal manifestations of, 45,
    compared to religious experiences, 133
    description of, 134-135
    levels of, 159
    as opposed and compared to Cosmic
        Consciousness, 131
    primary characteristic, 152
    relation to Objective Morality, 135
    reports of, 131-135
    techniques in ancient Egypt, 138-141
Objective Morality, 133
    definition of, 135
    first principle, 136
    five precepts of, 135-136
Objective view of Consciousness, 155
Objectivism, 2-5, 155-156, 157
    Behaviorist view, 3-4
    Burr's view, 4-5
Objects of active awareness, 38-39
Observation, processes of, 13-14
Octavic pattern of anabolism, 75, 85-86,
    102, 104-105, 108-109
Orage, Alfred Richard, 7, 100, 122, 124
Oral food, 76-77, 82, 83-85, 102, 105,
    108-109
Organic and inorganic matter as viewed
    by Objective Consciousness, 141
Organic energies, during Sleep, 71-80
    in Waking state, 72
Organic field, functioning of, 103
Original thought, in Waking state, 91
Osir, 145-146
Ouspensky, 97

Paradic, definition of, 46
Paradic emotional responses, 135
Paradic progression of conscious states for human beings, 51
Paradic sequence of behavior, 27
Parallelism, 2-3
Parallelist view of consciousness, 155-156
Partial conditions of Sleep, 53-54
Participation, technique of, 127
Passive consciousness, 20-27
  attributes of, 22-27
Passive vs. active impressions, 105-106
Passivity, as characteristic of un-awakeness, 17-27
  in Waking state, 85-97
Past civilizations, contribution to psychological thought, 8
Pavlov's theory of Sleep, 62
Perceptions, alterations of in Awakeness, 119-127
Phaulophilia, 48
Phenomena of consciousness, 2-3
Pièron theory of Sleep, 61
Portal vein, 76
Potentialities, Awakeness and Objective Consciousness seen as, 167
  real and unreal, 167
Practical man, as abnormal state, 86-87
Prescribed area for manifestations of organism in active awareness, 39
Problem of consciousness, analysis of, 11-27
Prohibition of thinking, 37
Protoplasm, electromagnetic properties of, 83
Pseudo-Sleep conditions, 158
Psychic qualities as defined in physical terms, 152
Psychological phenomena, 2-3
Psychological theories, 2
  objectivism, 2
  parallelism, 2-3
  subjectivism, 2-3
Psychonic energy, 4
Ptah, 144-146
Pulmonary circulation, 76, 82, 112

Rationality as distinct from practical logic, 69
Rationalization in Waking state, 88
Rationality of voters, 48
Re', 143-144
Receptors, response, in Sleep, 47

Reduction of consciousness in Sleep,
Reflexes during Sleep, 55, 66-67
Reinforcements of anabolic process, 75-
Relation between experiencer and neur raw material, 13
Relationship between neural event a subjective experience in Wakin state, 90
Religions, Egyptian, 137-141
  of Waking state, 138-139
Respiration, during Sleep, 57
Reversal of sequence in stage of behavi 26-27

Salmon theory of Sleep, 61
Science, attitude of toward universe, 14
Scientific method, steps in, 11
Scientific observations, fallacies of Waking state, 139-143
Scrutiny, as technique of consciousnes 41
Self Consciousness, in Bucke terminolog 133
Self-identification, 13-15
  See also Self-remembering.
Self-observation, technique of, 41
Self-remembering, 37-38
  Ouspenskian, 95
  technique of, 128
Sensation, 4
  categories of, 33-34
  as neurological event, 5
Sensations of muscular tension, types o 33
Sensory adaptation, in Waking State, 9
Sensory experience, 16-18
Sensory impressions as necessary to lif 105
Shock, function of in anabolism, 75, 7 82-85, 102-103, 109, 151
"Silent" areas in cerebellum, 66, 107, 11
"Sins", as lack of awareness, 138
Skeletal musculature during Sleep, 54
Skepticism as necessary attitude, 100
Skin resistance during Sleep, 57
Sleep, 45-47, 54-80
  abnormalities of, 47-48
  blood characteristics during, 56
  body temperature in, 55
  causes of, 60-71
  characteristics of paradic state of, 7
  circulatory system in, 56-57
  data on, 46-47

DC field alterations during, 59
definition of, 46, 54
digestion during, 55
E.E.G. during, 58
function of arrival platforms of cortex in, 47
as general, not local condition, 70
generic design of, 47
glandular system in, 56
heart action during, 56
as "instinct," 62
levels of, 53-54
magnetic disruption in, 70-71
organic activity in, 47
physiological symptoms, 54-80
as primal condition in Kleitman's theories, 65
prime characteristic, 53
receptors in, 47
reflexes during, 55, 66-67
relation of individual to environment in, 47
respiration during, 57
skeletal musculature during, 54
skin resistance during, 57
stages of, 157
theories of, 60-80
eep centers, 63
eeping-waking rhythm theory of Sleep, 65-66
Smoothing" of experiential content, 93
ocial consequences of passive consciousness, 97
olar plexus, in anabolic transformation, 85
oul, in ancient Egyptian belief, 138
pinal cord system, 86, 114, 160
in Sleep, 69, 70, 71, 77
in Waking state, 86
tates of consciousness, 45-51
Awakeness, 99-129
Objective Consciousness, 131-153
part vs. whole reaction in, 53
Sleep, 45-47, 54-80
Waking, 48-49, 81-98
teady-state electrical fields of living systems, 83
teiner, Rudolf, 3
tevenson theory of Sleep, 61
triped musculature, condition in Sleep, 47
ubconsciousness, 94

Subjective activity as key to energy transformation, 162-167
Subjective factor, effect of on energy transformation, 115-118
Subjective images, in Waking state, 92
Subjective view of Consciousness, 155
Subjectivism, 2-3, 155-156, 157
Suggestibility in Waking state, 48, 82
Sun, attributes, of, 140-145
Egyptian view of, 141-145
Waking state view of, 142
Sympathethic and parasympathetic theories of Sleep, 61
Synaptic connections, 17-19, 67
Synergy, 107, 112, 113

Techniques of active awareness, ancient Egyptian, 41
dangers of, 42, 164
defining characteristics, 35-43
excludes criticism, 35-36
excludes tutorialness, 36
Gnostic, 41
at Gurdjieff Institute, 41
in Io state, 33-43
necessity for companionship in practicing, 120
non-identification with organism, 37-38
not confined to special time or place, 39-40
prohibits analysis, 36
self-remembering, 37-38
Tehut, 145
Telepathy, credibility, 132
Thalamus, function of, 17, 63, 66, 67, 106-107
Theories of Sleep, 60-80
Thermodynamics, law of, 140
Third category of food supply, 102-105, 107-108
Thought, in Waking state, 90-91
Thought process, 4
difference from consciousness, 32
Threshhold of passive consciousness, 23
Transformation of energy, 74-80
Transformation of Io to I, 29-35
Triad, in Egyptian religion, 145
as universal phenomenon, 145-146
Tutorialness, exclusion of in awareness techniques, 35

U-curve of activity in Sleep, 69-71
Universe, as alive, 141-145
    Egyptian view of, 140-145
    inhabitants of in ancient Egyptian religion, 146
    Objective Consciousness view, 140-141
    Waking-state view, 140
Utilization of cerebral energy output, 107

Verbalisms confused with neurological reality in Waking state, 92
Vestibular reflexes, 112
Vestibular system, 107, 112, 113

"Wake", definition of, 81
Wakefulness centers, 64
Waking state, 34, 81-97

as abnormal condition, 81-82
abnormalities of, 48-49
AC brain waves in, 81
attitude toward universe in, 140
characteristics of, 48-49
DC tracings in, 81
delusions in, 89-97
digestion in, 72-76
disharmonies in, 86-97
functioning of divisions of nervous system in, 86-87
pathological conditions of, 158
religions of, 138-139
stages of, 158
three types of human distortions, 86-87
uneven energy expenditures in, 49
Watson, John B., 3
Wortis theory of Sleep, 61